Comments on other *Amazing Stories* from readers & reviewers

WILDLIFE IN THE KITCHEN

AMAZING STORIES

WILDLIFE IN THE KITCHEN

...And Other Great Animal Tales

ANIMAL/HUMAN INTEREST
by Roxanne Willems Snopek

PUBLISHED BY ALTITUDE PUBLISHING CANADA LTD.
1500 Railway Avenue, Canmore, Alberta T1W 1P6
www.altitudepublishing.com
1-800-957-6888

Publisher	Stephen Hutchings
Associate Publisher	Kara Turner
Series Editor	Jill Foran
Editor	Deborah Lawson

We acknowledge the financial support of the Government
of Canada through the Book Publishing Industry Development
Program (BPIDP) for our publishing activities.

Altitude GreenTree Program
Altitude Publishing will plant twice as many trees as were used
in the manufacturing of this product.

We acknowledge the support of the Canada Council for the Arts which
in 2003 invested $21.7 million in writing and publishing throughout Canada.

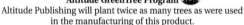

National Library of Canada Cataloguing in Publication Data

Snopek, Roxanne
Wildlife in the kitchen and other great animal tales / Roxanne
Willems Snopek.

(Amazing stories)
Includes bibliographical references.
ISBN 1-55439-008-7

1. Wildlife rehabilitators--Canada. 2. Wildlife rehabilitation--
Canada. I. Title. II. Series: Amazing stories (Canmore, Alta.)

SF996.45.S64 2005   639.9'6'0971
C2005-901167-X

An application for the trademark for Amazing Stories™
has been made and the registered trademark is pending.

Printed and bound in Canada by Friesens
2 4 6 8 9 7 5 3

To the many people who selflessly use their abilities and expertise to rescue and rehabilitate wild creatures injured by human activity. The world is a better place because of you.

Contents

Prologue

By the time she was dropped off at the wildlife shelter it was too late. Dried blood stained her bristly white guard hairs, matting the dark fur below. The lips above the long narrow muzzle were pulled back in a final grimace, exposing daunting canine teeth. She was a young opossum, hit during a nocturnal roadside ramble by a passing motorist. She'd dragged herself to cover at the side of the road but it was probably hours before a kind-hearted Samaritan found her and rushed her to the shelter. Now, as early morning sunshine streaked the sky, the last spark of life left her broken body.

Elizabeth laid her out on a soft towel and examined her quickly. Time was, after all, of the essence. The prehensile tail lay still, its furless skin cool to the touch. Eyes once dark and glistening now stared sightlessly, half-closed and dull. The woman manipulated the limbs, now flopping limply, felt through the fur over the soft, still-warm abdomen, searching, probing. There. That's what she was looking for.

Through a vertical opening in the opossum's belly, she felt a quiver of movement: babies. They'd survived the impact. She gently removed them from their mother's body and laid them in a warming basket, tiny pink hairless creatures no bigger than mice. She shook her head. They were living embryos, needing the warmth, security, and rich milk found within their mother's pouch for several more weeks at least. Could she give them what they needed? Or would they suffer the same fate as their mother?

She gave a last stroke to the dead mother and turned her attention to the living. She'd done it before. With any luck, she'd do it again. But these babies were so young; could any of them become strong enough to make it back to the wild?

All she could do was try.

Chapter 1
Baby Season in the Bird Ward

t's spring once again, the time of year when fledglings venture out of the nest, on their own for the first time. At Elizabeth's Wildlife Centre in Abbotsford, British Columbia, Elizabeth Melnick makes her way through a maze of flight cages, caring for babies whose first journey might very nearly have been their last.

A tidy outbuilding adjacent to her home houses her primary clinic, the treatment area where the most seriously injured birds and animals are cared for. She bends over a baby incubator, opens the porthole, and strokes a miniscule killdeer chick. "This one came in weighing 6 grams," she says, reaching for an insulin syringe minus the needle. She pulls a slurry of food mixture into the syringe and holds it above the gaping maw of the orphan. He gulps it down greedily, cheeping for more, but that's all he gets for now.

Next in line are two baby waxwings. "These birds are 90 percent fruit-eaters," she says, "so they get a mixture of canned puppy food, vitamins, strained blueberries, and applesauce." Her ability to recognize different species of birds is just as important as knowing their dietary requirements. Like human infants, many of them look very different from their adult counterparts but, unlike humans, they can have vastly different nutritional needs. There's no such thing as generic baby bird food. "People phone me up and ask what to feed this baby bird they found," Elizabeth says. "I try to get them to bring it to me instead, because I know it's probably going to die."

Few people know it's against the law to confine a wild animal for longer than 24 hours, even for the purposes of helping it. Elizabeth's Wildlife Centre Society is a licensed facility, with special permits from the British Columbia Ministry of Environment, Lands and Parks, as well as the Canadian Wildlife Service, that allow her to care for injured wildlife. The permits are necessary because the animal is the one who pays the price for amateur rescue attempts. Elizabeth regularly attends courses in wildlife rescue and is a member of numerous organizations for professional "rehabbers." Unfortunately, when people happen upon a wild animal or bird that needs help, they often want to try to save it themselves, maybe to keep as a pet, maybe simply for the inherent romance.

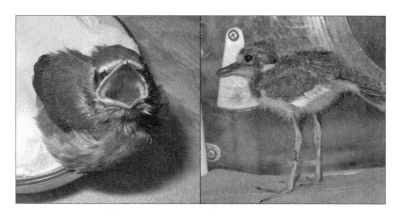

Patients at Elizabeth's Wildlife Centre:
(l) a cedar waxwing fledgling; (r) a baby killdeer

But the romance wears off quickly when the creature doesn't respond. "I'll get calls from people who have had a bird or a bunny or a squirrel for a couple of days, and it's not doing well," Elizabeth says. "By the time they bring it to me, it's nearly dead."

Elizabeth is very careful to make sure she meets or exceeds every requirement for her facility. Being in a residential subdivision, the last thing she needs is complaints from her neighbours. So her heart sank one day when one of her neighbours approached her to ask if she'd recently released a jay. Steller's jays, commonly seen west of the Rocky Mountains, are intelligent, beautiful birds with deep black-blue plumage, but they are raucously loud and can be persistent thieves. Elizabeth cringed to think that perhaps a bird she'd cared for might be becoming a neighbourhood pest.

The neighbour explained that her husband liked to go out onto the deck and enjoy a cigarette in the evenings. But recently, a jay had swooped onto the deck, snatched the cigarette out of his hand and flown to the roof with it. Elizabeth closed her eyes in horror at the image, envisioning the whole block of houses going up in smoke, but the neighbour quickly reassured her that the cigarette had gone out and the roof hadn't caught fire. "She told me that now her husband takes a piece of bread outside with him and the bird lets him finish his smoke in peace. Thank goodness!"

But she can't always predict her neighbours' reactions. "I had a little bantam rooster once," she says. "He was just a baby but then he started to crow, a really awful, pathetic noise." She knew once this jaunty little bird properly found his voice he'd be crowing at the break of dawn each day and that his urban neighbours might begin thinking he'd be a lot cuter in a pot. So she found him a home on a farm. Before she knew it, though, neighbours were asking her what had happened to the rooster. They'd enjoyed the morning serenade and missed it! "They told me that the next time I get a rooster I'm supposed to keep it," she comments wryly.

Elizabeth continues around the side of the building to where the stronger birds convalesce. In one cage, a grosbeak with a bad leg hops awkwardly from perch to perch, a jay with no tail waits for new feathers to come in, and a robin drags a damaged wing. Without protection predators would easily pick off each of these birds, but a little time to heal will give them a chance to make it. Five young pigeons coo and cluck in the next cage. "See the fluff on their heads?" she points out. "They're still babies." Three juvenile wood ducks rest quietly together in a shady pen beneath the shrubbery. Many of these birds are just here for a brief stopover to rest and regain some strength. "I released eleven yesterday," she says. "It's really quiet right now. It's like a holiday for me."

A total of 87 wild animals and birds reside in her shelter at the moment, during this "lull" in activity. "Sometimes I have 60 calls a day," Elizabeth says of the busy times. "I'll be running all day long." A slight, energetic woman, with bird-like quickness of movement, she confesses that she'll often lose 10 or more pounds when rescue season bursts to life in early spring and doesn't begin to gain it back until the temperatures drop and migratory birds leave for warmer climes. Each and every creature that enters her centre is recorded in the logbook, and she makes note of every telephone report of an animal or bird needing help. "I usually stay up until 1 a.m. or 2 a.m. working on records and logbooks," she says. "But I don't get up until about 8 a.m., so that's okay."

After the work involved in caring for the individual birds and managing the shelter, her next most important task is educating the public on what should and should not be done for wildlife. Each person she talks with is one less person who will inadvertently harm a baby bird, thinking it needs help. Baby birds found on the ground, she explains, are often simply at the beginning of their training. "They have to learn to fly from the ground up," says Elizabeth.

It's a natural stage of development where the young birds strengthen their muscles, she says, and the parents are vigilantly guarding them. Unfortunately, people spot the ungainly babies hopping around, and think they've fallen down and are helpless. They wave off the parents to pick up the youngsters and put them into a nearby nest, but the birds soon hop out again.

Elizabeth suggests that before approaching an apparently orphaned baby bird, people should first check to see if it appears injured. Is it hopping around? Does it have feathers? Is it really alone? Look around the area. Chances are, the parents are watching from a nearby perch. Finally, make sure there are no cats or dogs waiting to pounce on the baby. If it appears healthy and there are no predators stalking it, the best thing is to leave the young bird exactly where it is and let its parents tend to it. "As long as it can hop and has good feathers, it's going through a natural learning process," she summarizes.

Whenever possible, Elizabeth does what she calls a "soft-release," giving the birds a protected area in which to readjust to the great outdoors and freedom before setting them loose for good. At the back of her property is the pre-release flight cage, tucked next to a lush belt of deciduous and evergreen trees, salmonberry bushes, blackberry vines, and salal. Full-height, the cage is furnished with a variety of branches and twigs, allowing the birds to practise their take-off and landing skills in safety.

Once Elizabeth is sure they've got the skills they need to survive, she packs them into a transport cage and takes them to a protected area where they can start over again, in the wild. "We try and release the birds early in the day," she says, "when their food sources will be most plentiful." Release sites are carefully chosen based on the needs of the birds. Robins, for instance, can be fiercely territorial. Young robins released into an area already claimed by adults might be at risk of attack.

• • •

Jackie Ward, team leader of animal care at the Wildlife Rescue Association of BC, in Burnaby, British Columbia, remembers the large male Canada goose brought to their animal care centre one spring. A concerned passer-by had noticed him at the side of the road, injured and unable to get out of the way of traffic. Somehow, the man managed to capture the large bird and transport it to the shelter. "He'd likely been hit by a car," says Jackie. "He had soft tissue damage to his leg — nothing major but he was too sore to walk. He needed time in a protected environment."

Although many Canada geese are accustomed to the presence of humans, sometimes even dependent on them for food, captivity is extremely stressful for them. Many are so upset they refuse to eat. Because this gander's injury was relatively minor, everyone had high hopes for his quick recovery and release. But after a couple of days at the shelter, it became apparent that his convalescence was not going well; the bird wasn't eating or drinking and he seemed depressed. Instead of the steady improvement they expected to see, his condition was deteriorating quickly. They checked him carefully for additional injuries that might have been missed on the initial examination but found nothing. This mysterious malaise seemed to be caused by something else, something outside the realm of medical science. Staff members try hard to keep their emotions from clouding their judgment, but to several of the caregivers, he seemed to be pining, lonely. Was he missing his companions?

It was a reasonable theory. Canada geese are extremely social birds that form very close pair bonds. Once they mate, it's for life. Captive geese will honk loudly if they see others of their kind flying overhead, clearly wishing to join them. "When we've only got one in captivity, it can be very difficult for them," says Jackie. If this gander had been inadvertently separated from his mate, it would explain why he'd apparently lost his will to live. Several calls later, they discovered that after the male was brought in, a female goose had been seen in the same area, wandering around and calling. Could it be that the gander they'd been caring for was her mate? There was only one way to find out.

Jackie and her co-workers went to the area and set about

capturing the goose. That's when they discovered that not only had the gander been separated from his mate, but they had a clutch of goslings as well. No wonder he was anxious.

Many bird species are extremely protective of their young but none exemplify this like Canada geese. Both male and female Canada geese are very involved parents, and both are highly protective of the goslings. While the female tends to stay back and shield the young, the male is usually the more aggressive, actively chasing off threatening individuals. But this time rescue workers had to catch them in order to reunite the family. So they set out on a literal wild goose chase, rounding up mom and babies to go visit dad in the hospital. After much honking, hissing, cheeping, fluttering, and flapping, the noisy group was cloistered in a transport pen and loaded into the vehicle. They hoped they'd found the right goose; if it wasn't his mate, the gander could react with aggression.

But the instant the goose and goslings came near the pen where the gander was being kept, they knew they were witnessing a family reunion. The birds clustered and milled around each other, desperate to be as close as possible. "The change in the male was immediate," recalls Jackie. "They started to communicate once they were together again, standing in front of each other, lowering their heads and necks, opening their beaks, and making little noises." He was once more the picture of a strong, healthy Canada goose.

The best care in the world can't heal a broken heart. But when the heart is healed, everything else often follows suit.

With his family back again, the male's appetite returned, his energy level increased, and his leg quickly healed. Shortly after, the entire family was released back to the area in which they'd been found. The male flapped his wings and thank-lessly hissed at his caregivers, warning them away from his little family. But they understood. He was just doing his job.

Chapter 2
Wolf Watching

The gymnasium goes quiet. Over 100 kids sit cross-legged on the floor, wide-eyed, mouths hanging open. The object of their attention is the massive 50-kilogram wolf lounging casually on the stage next to his handler, Shelley Black. From the tip of his nose to the end of his tail, he measures about one-and-a-half metres. And he's only two years old, not completely full-grown. "This," says Shelley, "is Wiley." Wiley yawns, his cavernous jaw stretching to reveal a daunting set of gleaming white teeth, and the audience chuckles nervously.

Shelley and Wiley are from the Northern Lights Wildlife Wolf Centre in Golden, British Columbia, visiting the school to help educate children about the vital environmental importance of the wolf. Each presentation — to students as young as kindergartners — incorporates animal biology, ecology, sociology, plus the chance to meet a wolf, up close and personal! But before any face-to-face meeting occurs, Shelley makes sure all the children understand this is no ordinary house pet. "We cover all safety procedures with the students prior to introducing the wolf," emphasizes Shelley. The underlying principle is always to avoid triggering the wolf's innate predatory drive. In essence, children are taught not to act like prey — no running, no screaming or shrieking, and no sudden movements. Cooperation is rarely an issue but, just in case, Shelley adds a final caveat: *everything* is on the wolf's terms. The animal stays in the classroom only if the class behaves.

Then, and only then, does the lesson begin. Starting with the anatomy of a predator, Shelley teaches children about the special adaptations of wolves that make them good hunters. Then she describes the intricate relationship between predator and prey. "The wolf is classified as a key-stone species," explains Shelley. "Our goal is to teach people that we need the predator in the environment." Wolves, she continues, are at the top of the food chain. They prey on small mammals such as field mice, rabbits, and beaver, as well as larger animals like deer, elk, and other ungulates (hoofed mammals). This controls the populations of these animals, most of which eat only plant material. Without such population control, these species tend to increase in number until the land is overgrazed, trees and bushes are stripped, and, in short, the balance of nature is disrupted.

"In Yellowstone National Park in the 1950s, they studied this problem," says Shelley. "It started in the 1800s and by 1930 there were no wolves left in Yellowstone." The wolves were wiped out in the hope of protecting domestic livestock, as well as the wild ungulate populations. But what they discovered was that without the wolves, the park couldn't survive. Several dozen wolves were eventually brought in from Canada and reintroduced to the park. According to Shelley, a healthy wolf population checks the herds of herbivorous animals, which allows plants like willows and other trees to thrive, which in turn allows beaver to thrive and complete the circle by providing a food source for the wolves. Without a keystone species like the wolf, all of nature suffers.

Everyone is in favour of maintaining the balance of nature — in theory. But when faced with the real-life presence of wolves, many people react with raw fear, a type of panic that Shelley insists is unfounded. "There has never been a documented case of a vicious attack on a human by a healthy wild wolf, outside of captivity," she states. Fatal attacks by bears and cougars are common in North America, but there is no verified report of anyone being killed by a wolf. In every situation where a human has been injured by a wolf, she adds, there have been mitigating circumstances: captive wolves protecting a food source, a hurt or sick wolf acting defensively, or wild wolves that have been habituated to humans by thoughtless contact.

Wolves are characteristically secretive and will normally run away when they encounter people. Unfortunately, when well-meaning, curious, or ignorant wilderness visitors provide food and encourage the wolves to come ever-nearer for that elusive Kodak moment, the result is wolves that have become so habituated to human contact that they're no longer afraid of people. Such wolves are dangerous, to people as well as to themselves.

A tragic case on Vargas Island off the west coast of Vancouver Island in British Columbia illustrates Shelley's point most vividly. Populated by only a handful of permanent residents, Vargas is Clayoquot Sound's third-largest island, and one of the closest to the village of Tofino. The isolated island had long been a peaceful home for wolves. But when it was discovered as a beautiful destination for campers, day-trippers, and adventure seekers, things changed. As it became more popular with wilderness tourists, the wolves grew accustomed to the presence of humans. Instead of avoiding people, they became attracted to them — and the food they often offered. Local residents could do nothing but shake their heads. Year after year, the wolves took handouts from thoughtless picnickers and gradually their inherent fear of people turned to expectation.

It was a situation just waiting to go bad, and on one trip in the summer of 2000, it did. A group of kayakers had set up camp on the beach. During the night, a curious young wolf approached a camper sleeping on the beach and began nosing around, probably looking for food. The activity awakened the camper, who reacted with understandable alarm. When he yelled, he startled the wolf, and the wolf — just as understandably — reacted to defend himself. Then he turned tail and fled, leaving the man with severe facial and scalp lacerations that required dozens of sutures. But he was alive. "If the wolf had intended to do damage," says Shelley, "that man would be dead."

But fears ran high and intentions don't count in such situations. Conservation officers immediately went on the hunt, with the predictably tragic outcome. BC Parks put up signs at Vargas and other new provincial parks in Clayoquot Sound announcing: "People have been injured and wolves have been destroyed. Don't be the next victim!" The notices claimed that wildlife had "suffered the consequences of people's actions."

It's heartbreaking — and preventable. That's where Wiley and his buddy Moab come in. "They are travelling ambassador wolves," says Shelley. "Their job is to help save their cousins in the wild."

When Shelley and her husband, Casey, first set up their centre it was for the explicit purpose of teaching people about wolves, and about how humans and wolves can co-exist on the same planet. But their own education started much earlier. Casey had worked for many years as an animal wrangler for the film industry. "He did some training," says Shelley, "but mostly he cared for wolves and the other animals used in the movie industry." His knowledge of wolf behaviour began there but soon he wanted to take it further. And in a different direction. Instead of using wolves for entertainment, he wanted their wolves to play a role in educating people about wild wolves and how we can protect them.

"Our minds got changed," says Shelley. "We learned about other places that were teaching wolf awareness and we thought, 'We're in the Rocky Mountains, near Banff and Lake Louise, it's the perfect opportunity for us.'" They decided to do something to change public opinion and today they make their living working to keep wild wolves alive and safe in their natural habitat.

"We are an interpretive centre," says Shelley. "We have five wolves, all born and raised in captivity for the movie industry." Aspen, their first wolf, is actually a wolf hybrid, one-quarter husky, three-quarters grey wolf. She was a year old when Maya and her big brother Tuk arrived. From the beginning, the Blacks focused on giving their wolves the best life possible and making sure they would be safe around visitors. "Ours are the only wolves in the world that go for walks," says Shelley. "They go on trails outside the compound, off-leash, for 2 to 3 hours at a time."

A few years later, 10-day-old Wiley joined them and the Blacks discovered the joys of hand-rearing an infant wolf. It apparently agreed with them because in May 2004, the youngest member, Moab, joined their pack. The offspring of a white arctic wolf mother and a grey-brown male wolf from

Quebec, he arrived at the centre at the tender age of 24 days, weighing a mere two kilograms. Bottle-fed on goat's milk, little Moab received constant nurturing from both his human caregivers and his adopted wolf family.

By the time Moab was 10 weeks old, he'd more than quadrupled in size. Shelley and Casey had exposed him to people with extreme care and diligence, hoping he would become a valuable tool in their educational school programs. And it seems to have worked. "Weighing 10 kilograms, he is 50 centimetres high at the shoulder, and 75 centimetres long from nose to bum," says Shelley. "He has already met hundreds of schoolchildren from British Columbia and the United States, and hundreds more people from around the world."

With their mandate of conservation, Shelley and Casey Black are meticulous about doing everything right. "We do have a functioning wolf pack," says Shelley. "We have created our compound so that they aren't separated; they live together like a wild pack would live." The wolves live on one-and-a-half acres of fenced woodland, and they go outside the compound regularly with their human escorts. "At least two to three times a week the wolves go for a hike," says Shelley. "We go from one to four hours depending on the day and we only take two at a time — maybe three now, with Moab in training."

But no matter how well these wolves are cared for, the Blacks are quick to point out that it's not a natural life, and any puppies born to them would only end up in captivity. This is a prospect they refuse to consider. "All our animals are born in other zoo facilities," says Shelley, "and all are spayed and neutered."

So their little pack of five, plus Shelley and Casey, functions as a reasonable facsimile of a wild wolf pack. Wolves are among the most social animals in the world, and their lives revolve around the extended family of the pack. Wolf packs typically include a dominant pair, their offspring (including older pups from previous litters), and aunts and uncles of the young. The number of wolves in a pack is directly dependent upon the food available, and pack members co-operate in hunting and caring for the next generation.

Social structure within the wolf pack, as in many other animal groups, is strictly organized on the basis of a dominance hierarchy. And when it comes to dominance, size matters! Dominant wolves are unmistakable: everything about them appears large and formidable. They carry themselves tall and erect. Their ears are up and forward. Their tails are carried high on their backs. Because Aspen was full-grown when Tuk and Maya arrived, she naturally assumed the role of alpha wolf, or leader. Even though they've now outgrown her, Aspen remains the dominant wolf. None of the others question her authority. Wolves lower in the social order have very different body posture. They lower their bodies, tuck their tails and put their ears back. "Maya has always been the most submissive of our pack," says Shelley. "In the wild she would be called the 'beta wolf.'"

The main difference in this little pack is that, even for

Aspen, the ultimate leaders are the humans. "We act a lot like the alphas would in the wild — showing them food sources, protecting them, and making decisions for them," says Shelley. "We have raised them all from pups. Plus we control their food, and that has a lot to do with why they look up to us as the alpha pair."

Wild wolf packs have two separate hierarchies, male and female, and aggression is generally directed toward same-sex wolves. In a pack, everything — rank, food, the right to mate — comes with the price tag of competition. Wolves who lose such competitions can be driven out of the pack or even killed. For a wolf, being alone means being vulnerable to starvation. Most solitary wolves skulk hopefully at the edges of other packs, looking for a chance to once again be part of a family. "In over six years we've learned the social behaviour of the wolves, and we explain to people how similar it is to that of humans," says Shelley.

The wolf's co-operative nature is most strikingly demonstrated in pup rearing. Virtually all pack members contribute in one way or another. Pups are born helpless and utterly dependent, weighing about half a kilogram. The mother spends most of her time in the den with the pups for the first week. They need their mother not only for nourishment, but to regulate their own body temperature. With her every absence their tiny bodies become chilled; if she's gone long enough the puppies will die of hypothermia. When Wiley and Moab arrived at the centre as tiny pups, it was Maya, the submissive one, who stepped in as caregiver. "Maya's maternal instinct is strong, and she has taken on a protective and nurturing role," says Shelley.

Because puppies represent their future, pack members hunt and bring back food, allowing the mother to spend her time snuggling and feeding the new babies. Other females also nurse pups, sometimes even competing for access to them. If more than one litter is born, all surviving pups are usually put into one combined litter, tended and nursed by all the mothers.

When Wiley arrived at the centre, Maya immediately began digging him a sleeping area. When Moab was added to the family, Maya did what many parents do: she renovated, digging another den for the baby. "Maya was extremely loving to all our pups," says Shelley. "She became very possessive of the pups and didn't even allow me to be close to them. I think that that female would have lactated if she could have!"

When Moab was introduced to the pack upon his arrival at Northern Lights, the older wolves all eagerly sniffed at him through the fence, even before Shelley and Casey brought him inside the enclosure. Their responses were as individual as they are. "Aspen tolerates little ones," says Shelley. "Tuk keeps his distance, but he's the first one to regurgitate food for a new puppy."

Wolf pups develop rapidly and start venturing out of the den at about three weeks of age. At this time the other pack members, including adult males and yearlings, begin to help feeding them. In the wild, young wolves don't accompany the adults on hunting forays so the adult wolves carry food back to the den from a kill the only way they can: in their bellies. They gorge themselves on the kill then return to feed the younger wolves by bringing up the partially digested food. Even though this isn't necessary, thanks to their human caretakers, the adult wolves at Northern Lights still do their part to make sure the youngsters get sufficient nourishment. "When the pups are really young the adults don't hold back at all," says Shelley. This usually continues until the puppies are about three or four months old, but some wolves have an overly developed sense of responsibility. "I have witnessed Tuk regurgitate for Wiley when Wiley was a year and a half old," she remarks.

The mother usually resumes hunting after the pups emerge from the den and will often leave them alone or in the care of other pack members, sometimes yearling "babysitters," while she's out. All pack members seem to greatly enjoy playing with and caring for pups. "Wiley was a nervous and gangly teenager at first, forgetting where his feet were and stepping on the pup a few times," says Shelley. "Now he is rather like a big brother and spends half the time playing, and the other half trying to get away from a pesky young brother."

Even with this tender, loving care, only about half of all pups born in the wild survive to their first birthday. Shelley and Casey are grateful for the privilege and responsibility of raising their wolves, but they've earned it. To keep wild animals in captivity requires special licences. They pay several hundred dollars per animal, per year, to maintain their status.

The feeding alone of wolves is a formidable task. Northern Lights wolves are fed a variety of food, much of it donated from hunters, farmers, and ranchers. Wild wolves eat when they can, depending on the availability of prey and their ability to hunt successfully. To simulate life in the wild, the Blacks only feed their wolves every second day, and each wolf consumes 5 to 10 pounds at a time. Their diet consists primarily of wild game, but they also get beef, chicken, bison, and, for a treat, dry dog kibble. "Nothing is fed alive," emphasizes Shelley. "We even use road kill — although we have to pay for it! A hundred pounds lasts approximately 48 hours between the four adults. They eat everything."

Wild wolves are naturally afraid of people, and so are captive wolves if they aren't socialized at a young age. Tuk and Maya received minimal human contact as pups and, as a result, they remain shy and aloof with strangers. "We use Tuk and Maya as prime examples of what wild wolves are like," says Shelley. Because of their early hand-rearing by Shelley and Casey, Wiley and Moab are familiar with humans, making them the best candidates for public relations. "We allow kids to see just how large they are. We talk about the centre but the kids get to touch the wolves." Being face to face with a creature so close to the wild stimulates unbelievable reactions from the kids. "Some of the kids are scared, some are just amazed," she says, smiling. "Even the adults' reactions are pretty cool."

It's an unforgettable experience and that's what the Blacks are counting on. The more people that learn to care about wolves, the better their chances for survival in the wild. "In all of Canada," says Shelley, "wolves are not protected outside of parkland. A wolf gets less respect than a rat. They are officially classified as vermin."

The Blacks are passionate about wolf conservation. Watching the antics of their little family, it's easy to see why. "After living with them and being with them all the time," Shelley comments affectionately, "they grow on you."

Chapter 3
Lionheart

The feathery touch of a breeze stirred the pampas grass, nudging the lazy air, but only for a moment. As soon as the zephyr died the air settled again, onto a still plain crackling with heat. Against the setting sun the expanse of grass quivered like a calm, golden ocean, the smooth surface bewitching the unsuspecting zebra to come closer, closer.

Hidden within the grass the lion lay motionless, muscles poised, watching his prey. All nerves strained toward an unseen signal that would indicate the time had come. He waited, eyes and ears sorting information, preparing. His prey moved closer, almost within range. The lion shifted and leaned forward but it wasn't quite time yet. Wait a bit longer; let it get a bit closer. Patience, patience.

Suddenly, the moment arrived.

"Go!" urged the man beside the lion. The animal exploded into action; a predator had been unleashed. But would he be successful? The man ran behind, hoping against hope that this time the king of beasts would capture his prey. It was his only chance. Soon they would return to Canada and hunting season would be over forever.

Just east of Toronto, off the beaten track on the Old Kings Highway, tucked away in the little town of Bowmanville, Ontario, is North America's oldest private zoological park. Established in 1919, the Bowmanville Zoological Park (BZP) sprawls over 42 acres of gentle rolling hillside, mature shade trees, ponds, and meadows. It's home to over 300 exotic, non-human inhabitants. By day, zoo director Michael Hackenberger deals with the day-to-day minutia of administration, staffing, and public relations. But his true passion is training the animals, and the bigger the challenge, the better. The Bowmanville Zoo is a home for trained animals with "careers" in film and television. "This is the food for my soul. I love spending time with animals on this level. If I could do this 24 hours a day, I would. Instead," he says comically, "I have to be a crummy zoo director."

The BZP is an accredited member of CAZA, the Canadian Association of Zoos and Aquariums, and winner of the prestigious Thomas Baines Award for outstanding excellence and achievement, known to those in the field as the "Academy Award" of zoos.

But for Michael, pride has a much more poignant meaning. In early December 2001, four little bundles of fur were born, an unlikely and lasting legacy to Bongo, a lion who touched him in a way no other animal has.

When Michael got the call, over a decade ago, that the Ringling Bros. and Barnum and Bailey Circus in the United States had two young males they no longer needed, he decided to check them out. The cubs, born in the Maritimes at a now-defunct zoo, had been with the Ringling show until the circus obtained another big lion act. At 7 months of age, Bongo and Caesar were suddenly obsolete.

The tranquil, placid, unchanging scenery of a zoo can make it very difficult when animals, for whatever reason, must move to a new location. But Michael knew at first sight that Bongo and his companion Caesar were up to the move and would be coming home with him. He instantly recognized their potential suitability for the Bowmanville Zoo. "Right off the bat I saw big-boned, large-bodied, up-front animals," he recalls. "In captivity you often see poor quality animals but these were physically beautiful. And they were interested in people. I knew they were going to work." So Bongo and Caesar returned to Canada, the land of their birth.

"They were both superb animals genetically, with a well-laid basic foundation of training," says Michael. They'd also been very well socialized, something of a rarity in captive exotic animals. Michael knew these lions had what they needed to succeed on the world's stage. Or, as it turned out, to shine as stars of the big screen.

In 1996 Bongo and Caesar were chosen to play the title roles in the movie *The Ghost and the Darkness*, co-starring Michael Douglas and Val Kilmer. With great excitement, Michael and the lions embarked on a seven-month adventure in the Songimvelo Game Reserve in Mpumalanga Province on the border between South Africa and Swaziland. "I mean, taking lions to Africa," says Michael. "How does it get any better?" But challenges quickly appeared. Everything new was fascinating to the lions. Without the insight of native-born lions, they didn't see threats; the terrain was simply full of exciting things waiting to be explored. For Michael, this meant constant vigilance and another round of training for these big cats. If they discovered a spitting cobra under a bush, for instance, they needed to learn quickly that cobras are neither toys nor food.

Until then the training he'd done with the lions had been fairly regimented, focusing on accuracy and precision of movement. While this is perfect for live shows, on film it didn't look natural. "This type of training is of great benefit when you're working with potentially dangerous animals," says Michael, "but it made them look too choreographed. So I had to let go, behaviourally."

Bongo, who played the Ghost, had the majority of screen time and Michael had to step back and trust that Bongo could do what was required of him. "There are inherent risk factors," he admits, "but we had absolutely no issues on that level." Very few lions have been reliably trained to simulate viciousness against humans but even the breathtaking attack scenes came off without a hitch.

After a hard stretch of acting like a wild lion, Bongo got a fabulous reward: he got to go zebra-hunting. It was tremendously gratifying for everyone to see the animal they knew so well letting his inner carnivore have free reign. But rest assured, no zebras were ever harmed in the making of the film — or afterwards. "Bongo had a great time," says Michael, "but he was really bad at it. After he'd chase the zebras he'd lumber up to us for a scratch, looking all disappointed and sad."

The African people were fascinated by this white man and his Canadian lions. "We'd head into the townships with the lions in cages on the back of the pickups," recalls Michael. "I'd go in to get a Coke, and when I'd come back out there would be huge crowds of curious Africans, asking me to tell them about my lion." He opened the truck and had Bongo jump up on top of the cage so everyone could see him and he began to answer questions. Every time he spoke, voices immediately began translating into three different languages. "Where's he from?" they asked. "Canada," he answered. "Where's that?" "Far away in a land where snow falls on the ground," he explained. With disbelief and amusement, they responded, "No way!"

They were desperately poor people and yet their delight at seeing these strange lions was so great, they tried to pay Michael. "They wanted to give me a cow or a pig or a daughter," he says. "I had to insist that it was okay, there was no charge."

But one night near the end of the filming, he realized just how much impact these lions had had on the African people. Several thousand native labourers were hired as extras for the movie. They'd been working on the night sequences for three weeks, which meant trying to sleep during the full heat of the day. Work conditions were less than ideal; lighting up 20 acres required massive lights mounted on skyjacks, which attracted insects, which in turn attracted bats. Everyone was getting testy and frequent breaks for water and rest were essential. "I'm lying in the back of the pickup, with Bongo's head in my lap," remembers Michael. "The Zulu headboys came up to talk to me. They said they wanted to pay honour to me." Michael didn't quite know what this meant, so he responded by offering them passes to his zoo in Canada. But no, what they wanted was to touch him. "It's 45°C at night there," he says. "They touched my face and then wiped my sweat on their bodies."

Michael had no idea what to make of this. "I said to one of them, 'You gotta help me with this. I'm a Caucasian Canadian — what's this about?' They told me 'We've watched you, you work with lions, so you must have very strong magic.'"

Three days later the film was finally completed. Michael and the lions were on their way to the airport, eagerly anticipating their trip home. Michael was sitting on top of the cages as they pulled out onto the tarmac toward the plane. On top of the buildings, they saw armed guards watching them. "As I would go by they'd all clench their fists in the air," says Michael. While he was unhooking the cages, he commented to one of the helpers that the military must really think a lot of Bongo and Caesar. "It's you," the man corrected him. "'He Who Walks With Lions.'"

Michael will never forget the generous appreciation given him by the Africans, people who know lions as westerners never can. Even though his lions were born on Canadian soil, their hearts beat to the ancient rhythms of the jungle and their heritage is the savannah of their ancestors.

Everything that helps him understand his animals, allows him to train them more effectively. "I do all my training with positive food reinforcement," explains Michael. "Predators have an extremely well-developed food drive." Working for food rewards allows Michael to achieve an authoritative relationship with the animal without domination. "It's the equal relationships that are always the most appropriate and most successful," he says. "Both partners are bringing the same into it." He never forgets, however, that his work is extremely dangerous. "Whenever I am dealing with a large predator there are safety issues," he says matter-of-factly. "They kill other male animals to establish territory. You have to keep in mind, it's what they do. Don't take it personally." Knowing what makes the animal tick, he says, allows a trainer to predict behaviour, to see conflict before it erupts. It doesn't always work, he admits, but when problems arise, the responsibility lies squarely in the lap of the trainer. "Problems are of your own making," he emphasizes. "You know they're wild animals."

Michael speaks with the voice of experience. On a sweltering August night in 1998 Bongo was performing a show at Canada's Wonderland in Toronto. Even the most placid personalities in the troupe were getting a bit twitchy. The trainers were watching Bongo especially closely, as he always got a bit more contentious in summer. "Lions go through aggressive periods at around age four and age eight," says Michael. "In the wild, at four they'd be looking to take over a pride and at eight they'd be getting kicked out of a pride." Bongo was 10 but he appeared to be expressing that same sort of testosterone-driven territoriality, centred around — of all things — a roll of carpet.

The trainers had already used several tactics to try and get him away from the carpet and off the stage, but Bongo wasn't having any of it. He'd scarfed down the meat and bounded back to the rug before anyone could intervene. "I moved in and closed a couple of exits to contain the situation, but I could see that the carpet was his piece of earth to protect," says Michael. He put a pedestal in front of Bongo, to create a barrier between him and his object of desire. Usually this defuses the situation nicely. Not this time. Bongo rushed at Michael and before anyone knew what was happening, Michael's wrist was between those massive jaws. Later, Michael would learn that several bones in his wrist were cracked. But it was nothing compared to what Bongo could have done if he'd truly intended harm. It was a warning and Michael took it as such. He knew he had to keep his distance.

"I was about 20 metres away, farther than I've been with wild lions, when he charged me again." Bongo wasn't aiming for his hand this time; he was aiming for his face. Michael got the training pole in front of him and managed to push Bongo away but he knew there wouldn't be a third warning. "Next time, either I'd lose or he'd lose," he says. "I stepped out of the ring and we darted him." He'd been trying to avoid using the tranquilizer gun because Bongo had eaten about 30 pounds of food in their earlier attempts to mollify him. With a full stomach, even light sedation can lead to vomiting and choking. "So there I am, pulling food out of his mouth, and he's still trying to bite me," Michael remembers. He can laugh about it in retrospect; in 14 years with Bongo, it was his only scare and even then, Michael insists, it was his own fault. "Bongo was as honest as the day is long. He was never sneaky. Sure, he broke bones. But he could have killed me."

In most such situations intervention would have ended the conflict. This time, as soon as Bongo was recovered from the sedation and ready to rejoin the show he immediately ran to where the rug had been. He hadn't forgotten anything. But once he realized the rug was gone, he decided to give up the battle. Nothing else, it appeared, was quite worth fighting over.

In the summer of 2001, Bongo was being readied for

a scheduled trip to Argentina to film a commercial when Michael realized the big cat wasn't well. Some time earlier, Bongo had had a lump removed from his hip and he just hadn't bounced back from the surgery. They cancelled the trip and took him instead for MRI, magnetic resonance imaging. Unfortunately, Bongo turned out to be too big for the machine and they weren't able to do the procedure. But when they x-rayed his chest, the culprit was revealed: lung cancer. Bongo's time was quickly running out.

Michael was devastated. But that was when he made his toughest decision. He knew that if Bongo formed an attachment with a mate, he'd view all males — even Michael — as threats. Nevertheless, he decided to let Bongo live out his remaining weeks with a female lion, in the unlikely hope that Bongo's line would continue.

They chose a lioness from the Granby Zoo in Quebec, a young one that would be most likely to get along with Bongo. Because she was born at Granby during an ice storm, they had named her Gresil, a French word that loosely translates to "hail." Often known by her Anglicized name, Gracie, she quickly became Bongo's best friend, supplanting Michael for the first time in their relationship.

Bongo and Gracie were friends, but they didn't seem to be anything more than friends. It looked like Bongo's age and illness meant cubs weren't on his agenda. However, thanks to modern reproductive technology, there were other options. Bongo's caretakers collected semen for artificial insemination after his death.

In October it became apparent that Bongo's illness had progressed to the point where the majestic lion was no longer enjoying his life. "We'd set up a number of criteria," says Michael. "Loss of appetite, lethargy, that sort of thing. We knew it was time." Bongo died early in the morning, peacefully, surrounded by people who loved him. "It was a very sad period for us," says Michael. They'd been keeping the media informed about Bongo's deteriorating health and had released an announcement of his death to the press. "I was driving into Toronto that morning when the 8:30 news came on and they read about his passing," recalls Michael. "I pulled over and just bawled my eyes out." Michael may have been Bongo's closest human companion, but people from all over the world sent notes, flowers, and pictures when they learned of his death.

Shortly after Bongo's death they discovered he'd left one last surprise. Gracie was pregnant after all, the old-fashioned way, and in early December 2001, she gave birth to four cubs.

Today, a young male named Bowman stars in the shows at the Bowmanville Zoo. He looks just like his dad but he will never replace Bongo in Michael's heart. "I can count on one hand the great animals I've worked with," he says. "Bongo was a great lion. I can develop a lion so far but after that it's a gift ... Bongo was a gift from the gods."

Because of the great many lives Bongo touched, his final resting place is in an area of the zoo open to the public.

A tree grows above the stone that marks the spot. On the stone are these words: "He was a star. He was a king. He was our friend."

Chapter 4
Rock and Peep: A Love Story

In the backyard, the birds are just settling in for the night. The last feeding is finished and Joan Biggs is covering, closing, and latching the cages. Inside, on perches and branches, are songbirds of all sorts, from starlings, blue jays, and crows, to robins, cardinals, orioles, chimney swifts, and tiny finches. "We haven't had a hummingbird yet," says Joan. "But I know what to do when we get one."

Joan and Neil Biggs have been rehabilitating wild birds for the past decade and their For the Birds Sanctuary has the necessary licence and permits to ensure that birds passing through their Sarnia, Ontario, facility receive the best possible care. As a registered charity, there's a great deal of paperwork involved. "We have to report to Canadian Wildlife Services at the end of each year and tell them how many birds we've had, what type, how old they were, and what happened to them," explains Joan. "It's a lot of work." The administrative work is a hassle, but it's worth it because of the birds. She notes this with a certain pride because 10 years ago she couldn't have imagined feeling this way. "I didn't like anything flying or fluttering around me," she says. "Not even butterflies!"

Then one spring her husband, Neil, took care of a fledgling starling. "They leave the nest before they can fly and just need some assistance," she says. Neil sheltered the little bird until it was ready to fly off on its own and that was that. But word got around that he was someone who knew about wild birds; before long they were landed with an entire nest of starlings. Joan didn't know what to think. She felt sorry for the tiny orphans but it wasn't easy to let go of her squeamishness. "Then Neil told me I had to just get over it," remembers Joan. "So I did."

From then on she was hooked. They soaked up as much knowledge as they could — from other wildlife rehabilitators, from veterinarians, and from books and newsletters. But still, when Joan went to the Humane Society in response to their call about a baby bird, she didn't recognize the gangly, funnylooking creature they presented her with. "I said 'What's that?' and they told me 'It's a pigeon! Are you still going to take it?'" She and Neil had never cared for a baby pigeon before but she didn't hesitate, and the baby went home with her.

Pigeons, who belong to the same family as doves, are

sometimes known as rock birds or rock doves. While this family has a multitude of subspecies, the term *pigeon* usually refers to larger birds that have rather square or rounded tails, while *dove* refers to the smaller ones with pointed tails. The birds often seen roosting in the ledges of high buildings, commonly known as pigeons, recently had their name officially changed by the American Ornithologists' Union to *rock pigeon.*

The rock pigeon is one of the oldest domesticated animals, and was used as food by Egyptians as far back as 2600 B.C. In some Islamic countries pigeons and doves were protected on religious grounds.

The French introduced this bird into North America at Port Royal, Nova Scotia, in 1606. Rock pigeons have flourished throughout North, Central, and South America, the Hawaiian Islands, and parts of the West Indies. These birds naturally inhabit the rocky cliffs of coastal areas, so they find the ledges of high buildings a perfect substitute and have become abundant in cities, towns, and rural areas all over the world, wherever humans are close by.

Humans and pigeons, it seems, have a mutual attraction. Joan and Neil were about to learn just how strong this attraction could be.

Pigeon parents produce a very nutritious "pigeon milk" that they feed to their young by regurgitation. This baby bird would squeal for the substitute formula Joan and Neil had mixed up for her, its wings flapping rapidly above its head as it bowed down and drank from the notched baby bottle nipple. "We were always amazed at the amount this bird could drink," Neil says. "It would push along the table top trying to catch the bottle as we were taking it away, even though it was so weighed down by the fullness of its crop that we were afraid the crop would burst."

They had no way of knowing if their new baby was a male or a female, so they named it Rock. But the fledgling grew quickly and, before long, they began to suspect she was female. She had a definite personality — "avianality," according to Neil — and felt protective and possessive about what she saw as her territory. "We'd take her outside with us and watch as she chased other birds around the yard," says Neil. Rock was turning into a beautiful bird and they expected that soon she'd be ready to move out on her own. "We didn't really expect her to stick around," says Joan. "Our other birds usually joined the wild flocks that come by our house. But Rock didn't. She wanted to stay."

It wasn't long before the reason became clear: Rock was in love with Neil!

"We really don't know how she figured out which one of us was the male, but it became very apparent she saw me as a prospective mate and my wife as a threat," says Neil. Pigeons may not look intelligent or valuable, but they're commonly used in laboratory experiments in biology, medicine, and cognitive science. They can be trained to distinguish between cubist and impressionist paintings, for instance, and have been shown to be more effective than humans in spotting shipwreck victims at sea. "Rock was obviously smarter than me," says Neil sheepishly, "because for the first six months she was around, I was sure her belligerent, dominating ways indicated she was a male. How silly of me."

Rock's jealousy was unmistakable. She routinely flew at Joan, biting at her and pulling on her clothing, clearly trying to drive her away. Then she'd turn to Neil, bowing and cooing.

Joan couldn't help feeling a bit put out. After all her work with the bird she hadn't expected Rock to reject her so blatantly. "Here I lovingly cared for her and worried about her, and what does she do?" queries Joan. "She dumps me and goes for my husband!"

When Rock was old enough to move out of the house they decided it would be prudent to encourage some distance. It was time she realized Neil wasn't the one for her. "We set up a covered pigeon coop in the backyard with an opening big enough for her to have some freedom during the day, and a heat box for warmth at night," says Neil. But Rock wasn't about to let her true love go so easily. Back and forth she flew, from window to window, trying desperately to find a way inside the house, back to her chosen mate. "The whole neighbourhood was talking about that crazy pigeon's attempts to get into the house after we locked her out," says Neil. "She just didn't understand at all. She had selected me as her partner and now she couldn't reach me."

Around the same time, another fledgling pigeon arrived.

Peep, as they named him, was old enough to know he didn't want to be a pet. But he was still too young to care for himself; an adult pigeon's diet consists of fruits, seeds, berries, and small insects, but Peep wasn't quite ready for that yet.

It soon became apparent that young Peep was smitten with Rock. She, however, wanted nothing to do with him. He began to follow her around, lovesick and persistent, but all she could think of was finding Neil. "Whenever I had to go some place she'd follow me," says Neil. She'd land on the windshield wiper of his car and refuse to leave. Her persistence nearly caused her death many times, but she didn't even appear to notice. When he finally gave in and let her inside the car, she'd sit on the headrest beside him. "It was the only way not to risk her life," he says. "She would ride on the roof until the wind blew her off, then stare at the car from where she landed, which was usually the middle of the road." Neil would have to pull over and pick her up so other cars wouldn't hit her. Incredulous drivers slowed to watch. Neil was just glad he never caused a collision, stopping to pick up his lovelorn bird from the road. He watched one passing motorist try to drive while gazing open-mouthed at his unusual passenger. "I thought an accident was going to happen when a woman noticed Rock on the headrest as she was turning," he says. "I thought she'd go up the curb."

Peep continued to pay court to his lady-love and Rock robustly continued to remind him that not only was she not interested, but she also found him irritating in the extreme.

"When birds don't want anything around," explains Joan, "they flick their wings, like you do with a towel. Peep did his song and dance and Rock just wing-flicked him and then flew up to Neil. Poor Peep looked so dejected."

Eventually Peep's persistence wore her down and Rock decided to move into the nest box with him. "She followed me around for two years trying to entice me to her nest," laughs Neil. "Then she was reintroduced to the pigeon world by Peep. Finally realizing she wasn't human, she settled for second-best with her pigeon mate." She continued to fly down to sit with Neil whenever she could, but in time her attitude seemed to be that if you can't be with the one you love, love the one you're with. "Poor Peep didn't know what he was in for," says Neil. "It probably wasn't a normal pigeon relationship."

Apparently it was normal enough; before long, there were eggs in the nest. Both pigeon parents work to guard the nest and incubate the eggs, a process that lasts about 18 days and although she'd never done this before, Rock did her share. When the eggs hatched, however, it was another story altogether. "She stood up, stepped aside, and just looked at them as if to say 'What are these things and where did they come from?'" remembers Joan. Although pigeons also share parenting duties, that first time Peep did double duty while Rock went through a brief identity crisis. A couple of times Joan and Neil had to drag out the ladder and step in to make sure the babies were being kept warm enough. But before long Rock figured out her motherly responsibilities. As time went by, Rock settled into a routine with Peep and the wild pigeons in the neighbourhood.

And then Rock went missing.

Despite not being migratory birds, pigeons' outstanding homing capabilities have gained them a long and rich history of delivering messages, including during the times of Caesar and Napoleon. It's thought that they use magnetic fields to return to their home lofts, but this was cold comfort when Rock disappeared.

"A couple of times we thought we'd lost her because she didn't show up for a few weeks," says Neil. "I think one time somebody probably tried to keep her as a pet until they tired of her or she escaped." This time, though, she must have wandered farther than usual and been unable to fly back. Joan and Neil were grief-stricken, thinking she'd been hurt or killed. Even though Rock had so thoroughly rejected her, Joan wished aloud that the feisty pigeon would find her way home. "Within half an hour," says Neil, "I got a phone call from the Humane Society wondering if we would look after a rather vicious pigeon that needed time to regrow her flight feathers. I went outside and told Joan I was going to the Humane Society to pick up Rock." Joan didn't believe him. But Neil knew that since all the workers at the Humane Society were women, Rock wouldn't exactly be on her best behaviour. "I came out of the back room of the Humane Society with Rock riding on my shoulder, to an incredulous bunch of women saying, 'You're kidding, this is your bird?' I keep telling Joan to wish for riches," Neil teases, "because her wishes do come true sometimes."

Another spring arrived and now the little sanctuary had a flock of seven pigeons with more eggs under Rock. As spring wore on, their birds took to the air more and more and before long they were being accompanied by other pigeons from the wild flocks. "Our flock was growing in numbers," says Neil. "Luckily, Rock and Peep kept the rest from nesting at our place so our flock was a visiting one rather than a resident one." Of course, the more birds they had visiting their yard, the more food they needed to put out. The more food they put out, the more the birds visited. And the more birds they had, the more predators began to lurk in the background. "We ended up with hawks visiting the yard looking for easy prey," Neil commented soberly.

One evening near dusk Joan was working at her computer. Peep and Rock's nest box was just above the window near her desk. The birds were coming back to roost for the night when Joan heard a sudden thud, and saw feathers fluttering to the ground. With dread, she recognized the signs of a hawk attack and ran outside, hoping against hope that it wasn't one of their birds. "I kept thinking, 'Don't let it be them, don't let it be them!'" she remembers. "But it was Rock."

Pigeons mate for life. Even though Rock had never shown Peep anything in return, he had loved her with his entire being. Now Peep was grief-stricken. He mourned his lost mate for over a week, going between the peak of the roof and the nest box, calling for her and crying. "He just stood there and howled," says Joan. "This was no loving coo, it was more like a growl, but really loud and constant."

Eventually, Peep joined the wild flock. Once he left, he never returned to the nest box he'd shared with Rock and eventually he found another mate. "He brought her over and you'd see them both walking through the backyard, eating peanuts," says Joan. "He wouldn't live here anymore, but he'd still come back to visit."

For Neil and Joan, who'd raised their bold little bird by hand, the loss hit hard. The only consolation they had was that, of all the ways she could have died, this was the most useful. Hard as it was to think of, Rock's death helped bring life to a nest of young hawks somewhere. Her life hadn't been long, but it had been much longer than it would have been without human intervention. And she got to experience everything but growing old. Instead of starving to death as a baby, or becoming a cat toy due to bad molts, or becoming a slave in a cage for a well-intentioned human, Rock had fulfilled her destiny: living, flying, and breeding. Her three successful clutches meant that another six rock pigeons and their offspring fly around the Sarnia area, all of which still visit the Biggs' sanctuary for food, water, and a measure of safety in an otherwise harsh world.

In addition, Rock introduced Joan and Neil to another species of bird they might not otherwise have known. They happily take in other orphaned pigeons now. And when fledglings are ready to leave, the visiting flock is perfect for reintroducing them to the wild.

Rock will never be forgotten at For the Birds Sanctuary. "We still think of her often, and we have video, sounds, and pictures to remember her by," says Neil. "When we get nostalgic, we play the video of her attacking Joan and nuzzling up to me. I really wish I knew how she figured out I was the male." Rock brought laughter, love, and the reminder that things aren't always what they first seem.

Chapter 5
Saved at Sea

A booming crack slices the air. It sounds like a gunshot, but it's not. It's the spring ice break-up on the frigid waters at the mouth of the Churchill River, and it's music to the ears of Mike and Doreen Macri. They operate Sea North Tours in Churchill, Manitoba, where, when the warm sun of July and August finally drives the chill of winter from the water, beluga whales arrive in droves.

Beluga whales live in the arctic and subarctic regions of Russia, Greenland, and North America. Among all whales, only the beluga, the bowhead, and the narwhal spend their entire lives in arctic waters. Most beluga pods are migratory, heading north to the Hudson Straits in the fall when the ice forms and returning south to the river estuaries in the spring to feed in the warmer waters where river meets ocean. The return of the belugas always brings excitement to Churchill.

Mike has always loved the sea, and he and his wife Doreen are year-round residents of Churchill. Since 1977 they have turned this love into a business, specializing in marine tours. They take up to 30 tourists at a time out on their custom-made, 12-metre boat to look at whales, polar bears, pelagic (open-sea) birds, seals, and other marvels of the northern waters. But 24 years ago, Mike was just another whale-watcher. "I've always liked being around animals, especially whales," Mike says. "All week I'd be at work, but on weekends I'd be out with my dog on the boat." There weren't very many tourists then, but he often saw people standing on the rocks, looking at whales through binoculars. Now and then he invited them to come with him on the little 6-metre boat he had at the time. He enjoyed sharing his love of the sea and his attraction to these hypnotic cetaceans. And although it's never easy to predict where the belugas might be found enjoying a meal, if anyone could find them, it was Mike. "Word got around," he says, "and people started to pay me. Soon I was making more money on the weekends than I did at my job."

That's when he knew it was time to make a change. He needed a bigger boat, made especially with whale-friendly viewing in mind. So he consulted a naval architect and had one built. "It's propelled by jet pumps. No moving parts are exposed beneath the surface, so whales can come underneath without being harmed," says Mike. "It's quiet too, with very little underwater noise, so it disturbs the whales as little as possible."

As Mike discovered, beluga whales feed in open water and on the sea bottom, in the shallows and in the depths. They dine on a variety of sea-life, including capelin, a variety of crustaceans, plus small char, white fish, cisco, and sea-run speckled trout. An adult beluga consumes approximately 12 to 14 kilograms of food in a day. They may even have some sense of taste, but they don't have the brain receptors or olfactory structures for a sense of smell.

Belugas can grow up to six metres in length. So having a group of belugas within arm's reach is beyond exciting. When they're occupied with feeding they completely ignore nearby boats. But when they're not feeding, Mike and his passengers become *their* entertainment. "They come right under the boat," he says. "Last week nine of them took turns pushing the boat with their heads, scratching their backs on the hull." Is this just the whales' way of being super-friendly? Not exactly. During their annual summer molt, when belugas shed their outer layer of skin, they love nothing better than a good scratch. The bottom of anything that floats is just the ticket. Even after all these years, Mike still feels the excitement of it. "Especially on the zodiac," he comments. "You don't feel it quite so much when they're bumping the big boat."

Mike sees the whales every day, all summer long, from the time the first ones arrive in spring until the last ones leave in fall. "I still like watching whales, but what I really like is watching people see them for the first time," he says. "Some people scream. I think everyone's surprised there are so many of them, and that they get so close. People don't realize these things until they're actually in the boat, surrounded by the whales."

Female belugas and their young tend to favour areas of calm, shallow water with sand, gravel, and mud bottoms, while pods of adult males and females prefer deeper, colder waters. They can remain submerged for 25 minutes at a time and may travel 2 to 3 kilometres on one dive. And they're known to have excellent vision, both in and out of water. Belugas often travel in large groups. Mike estimates that, during whale season, anywhere from 2000 to 3000 of these magnificent creatures are in the area on any given day.

Beluga whales are sometimes called "sea canaries" because they are extremely vocal, and scientists speculate that the moveable, melon-shaped area on their heads is used in communication. Mike's boat is specially equipped with stereo-hydrophones, a type of underwater microphone, so his passengers can enjoy the whale sounds. No matter how often he listens to them, he always hears something different. "Whistling, chirping, sometimes they sound like chimpanzees or chickens or even cows," he says. "Yesterday there was this melodic whistling noise I'd never heard before. It was really quite nice."

Beluga whales are very social creatures, and a group of

them can be quite loud. Like bats, belugas use echolocation to identify and navigate their surroundings. Their underwater clicks and whistles bounce off objects in the water, giving the whales a sort of "sound-map" of their environment. These clicks have a distinctive static-like sound; divers and snorklers often know whales are nearby because of the unique physical sensation these sound waves create in their chests.

Besides sound, these whales have many other subtle forms of communication. They are unusual among whales in that they have full range of motion in their necks, allowing them to nod, shake their heads, and even look perplexed.

Although Mike watches them closely, it's difficult to identify individual whales. Belugas don't have dorsal fins, a helpful identification tool in other species, nor is there any colour variation among adults. The name "beluga" comes from the Russian word *belukha*, which means "white one." They're born dark grey and gradually turn white by the time they are anywhere from three to eight years of age. Unless they have deep scars or physical peculiarities, any identifying marks disappear when they shed their skin.

But there's one whale Mike would very much like to meet again.

"I was coming back from a tour one time," he recalls, "when I saw something white bobbing out in the bay." He had no idea what it was, so after he took the last tourists back to shore he headed back out to take a look. It turned out to be a bleach jug and beneath it was an arctic net. Jumbled up amongst the mesh Mike saw a young beluga whale, about 5 metres long, struggling for breath. "He was tangled up in the net," recalls Mike. "Occasionally he'd come up for air but the weights on the net kept dragging him down. He was drowning."

Unless they fall prey to killer whales or polar bears, beluga whales have a lifespan of 35 to 50 years. Their affinity for shallow coastal waters makes them vulnerable to dams, off-shore petroleum exploration and extraction, and the effects of pollution. Getting caught in ice or nets is often fatal as well, since it prevents these sea mammals from reaching the surface to breathe. Mike wasn't about to watch this one die as a result of a discarded net.

Arctic nets are made of thin but extremely strong monofilament. Mike knew that if he attempted to move the net, and the whale struggled, either he or the whale could be badly cut. He couldn't do much on his own so he raced back to shore, picked up a friend, and together they hurried to save the young whale.

For about five minutes, they held the net up high enough so the whale's blowhole was above the surface, allowing him to catch his breath. They hoped he wouldn't panic. "We knew that if this guy decided to go, we wouldn't be able to hang onto the net," says Mike. "It would rip our fingers off."

But the whale seemed to know they were trying to help. "I took my knife out with one hand and started to cut the mesh around his head," says Mike. "He was completely wrapped in it, right around to his tail." Mike continued cutting away at the net, working to free the animal from the mesh that bit deeply into his flesh in some places. Then he got to the tail, the trickiest part. If the whale began to struggle it would be dangerous for them all. To Mike's surprise, he let them continue cutting until the very last mesh thread was severed. "Then he very slowly started to move away," Mike says. "This guy had no problem letting us help him."

Mike may never know what became of this young beluga, but he'll always remember the silent plea in his eyes, and how honoured he felt that this desperate creature trusted him with his life.

• • •

In the tiny community of Kyuquot, situated at the very edge of the open ocean on the far west of the country, another ocean creature owes its life to human assistance.

No one reaches Kyuquot by accident. Getting to the village requires a four-by-four to cross the rough logging roads of northern Vancouver Island, followed by a boat or a seaplane. But in spite of these inconveniences, visitors still come to Kyuquot, lured by pristine wilderness and great fishing. When they do come, chances are they'll stop in at Miss Charlie's Restaurant and Lodging. Chances are they'll see Charlie, sunning her sleek 160-kilogram self on the dock of Walter's Cove.

And if they leave their salmon unattended on the dock, they might see Charlie helping herself to a snack, for Charlie is a seal.

Sandra Kayra, known to her friends as Sam, is the proprietor of Miss Charlie's and she never tires of telling people about her business's namesake. No one knows the story better than Sam does; she grew up with Charlie. About 40 years ago, she explains, the government paid a bounty for seals — five dollars per seal, a significant reward at the time — counted by the number of noses turned in. A group of seal hunters working their bloody trade in the area had a particularly macabre way of making an extra fee: when they came across an obviously pregnant seal they would remove the baby after killing the mother, and get two bounties for the work of one. Sam's mother, Lucy Kayra, knew of this practice and told the hunters that if they found such a seal, she'd pay the bounty herself, in return for the living pup. It wasn't the first time Lucy had cared for a wild creature. "Growing up," says Sam, "we had eagles, seagulls, mink, otter, anything injured or orphaned."

So in the summer of 1964, the Kayra family expanded by one 10-kilogram newborn seal pup. "We proceeded to pack her up and put her in the bathtub," remembers Sam. "We had a lot of the community in our bathroom that night!"

Lucy contacted the Vancouver Aquarium for advice and was given a recipe for a very rich, high-fat "baby" formula, suitable to replace the high-calorie, nutrient-dense seal milk.

"Mom would heat it up in a baby bottle — *my* baby bottle — and feed her," says Sam.

A visiting cousin named the seal Charlie and by the time they learned their little baby was a girl, the moniker had already stuck. But it didn't matter; the name Charlie suited her perfectly.

As Charlie grew, the family moved her outdoors and began teaching her the skills she'd need to survive in the sea. "Dad built a net-cage we could put in the water," says Sam. "He didn't want to just let her go without preparing her." By pulling the net-cage out a bit deeper each day, they helped their little seal learn to swim. "Mom taught her to catch fish," says Sam. "She put herring on a rope and let Charlie chase it, playing with her." Sam affectionately recalls the seal's rather picky eating habits. "Dad brought her salmon. She preferred sockeye — but Charlie only wanted it if it was filleted, and all the fins were off."

Charlie grew quickly and soon acquired the basic skills needed to live as a seal. But she never went far from her home. "She always hung around the bay, staying near the dock," says Sam. "She loved kids, and whenever she heard young voices she'd show up to swim with us. If we were paddling the canoe she'd come by and tip us out. She even considered herself something of a guardian; when other seals came into the bay, she'd chase them away from *her* people. She thought she was human."

But *her* humans were determined to let her live a

natural life and they expected that, as she reached maturity, she would be drawn to her own kind. They knew they'd miss her, but they wouldn't think of depriving her of a wild seal's life. So the first mating season after she was fully grown, Sam's father, Esko, packed Charlie into the boat, took her to a seal colony in the outer Bunsby Islands, about 16 kilometres to the west, and said goodbye. "There was a floating logging camp about a kilometre away, so Dad swung by and notified the loggers in case Charlie showed up, recognizing humans," says Sam. But she never did.

The bay was quiet without her and the dock seemed empty. Then, a full week later, Charlie swam her way into their lives again. "She looked tired when she arrived," says Sam, "but it was amazing that she found her way back to Walter's Cove."

Charlie, apparently, had made her choice.

In the nearly four decades she's been part of the Kyuquot community, the seal has become something of a mascot. Everyone knows her and everyone feeds her. Charlie, who used to slim down in the cold winter months, stays fat and healthy all year round now, thanks to the regular handouts she gets from her human friends. "She's now blind," says Sam, "and her hearing isn't as good as it used to be. But the local people love her."

Charlie has already lived longer than most seals will live in the wild. The 170 residents of Kyuquot know she won't be around for very many more years. But, taking pride of place on the walls of Miss Charlie's Restaurant and Lodging, photos are displayed of the seal that chose to stay. Clearly, the community will never let Charlie be forgotten.

Chapter 6
When Polar Bears Come to Town

Shrieks of laughter compete with the crunching of frozen ground under dozens of small, boot-clad feet as the late afternoon light wanes. Excitement mounts as more and more well-bundled youngsters fill the streets, anticipating the annual candy-fest of Halloween. But here in Churchill, Manitoba, something is a little different. In the sky above the haunted streets, a Jet Ranger helicopter flies a pre-dark patrol. Vehicles from Manitoba Conservation, the Royal Canadian Mounted Police, Churchill Ambulance, and Parks Canada prowl slowly from one street to another, throughout the entire small town. Churchill Volunteer Fire Department trucks and Canadian Ranger vehicles sit motionless, guarding the perimeter. Why, on this traditionally spookiest night of the year, does Churchill require such heightened awareness?

It has nothing to do with the supernatural. The town pulls out all the stops so that, on this one night, it will be safe for its children to be out after dark. It's the height of the polar bear migration — and no one wants them crashing the Halloween party. The helicopters, with Polar Bear Alert crew members on board, are simply advance scouts in the search for any polar bears that come too close to town. And any bear that poses a threat can expect a "trick" in the form of a tranquilizing dart.

Richard Romaniuk, district supervisor with Manitoba Conservation, has been with the department since 1983. This is his fifth bear season in Churchill and polar bears are his department's primary responsibility. "We protect people from bears and we protect bears from people," says Richard.

Churchill's relationship with bears is due to one simple thing: location. The polar bear, whose scientific name, *ursus maritimus*, means "sea bear," is found throughout the arctic seas. Churchill, on the edge of Hudson Bay, just happens to lie at the southern limit of their range. These bears, the world's largest land carnivores, truly are at home in the frigid northern waters. They can swim close to 100 kilometres at a stretch, equivalent to crossing the English Channel three times without a break. They can dive five metres beneath the surface and stay under for two minutes at a time. Underwater, they have the ability to close their nostrils and flatten their ears while keeping their eyes open to hunt. And it's not uncommon for them to leap two or three metres out of the water, straight up into the air, during a seal ambush. They'd happily stay on the sea ice all year long. But that's not an option for the polar bears of the Churchill region.

By the end of July or early August, the Hudson Bay ice melts, forcing the bears ashore. Instead of hunting during their stay on land, these huge bears wander lazily over the brushy tundra in what's called a "walking hibernation," burning off the fat reserves built up over the winter and conserving energy until they can get back out to sea. As summer wanes and the air begins to chill, they follow the banks of the Churchill River toward the salt water of the bay. By October they've gathered on the outskirts of town, waiting for the bay to ice over and give them access to the ocean once more.

Ice first forms along the western coast of Hudson Bay, and usually runs north along the coast from Cape Churchill. In the past, bears seldom made it further than the Fort Churchill military base, where they were shot on sight. But after the base closed down in the early 1970s they were free to continue on to the tiny town of Churchill. Throughout the fall, and especially just before freeze-up, increasing numbers of bears move toward the coast where they gather within easy viewing access of their human neighbours. Hundreds of them pass by or through Churchill during their fall migration, earning the town the title of "Polar Bear Capital of the World."

Fortunately, even during their migration, most polar bears prefer to avoid confrontation with people. These arctic

A polar bear on the Canadian tundra

giants have few natural enemies; they occasionally kill each other, and adult males will not hesitate to kill cubs if they get the chance. But for the most part, polar bears reign at the top of the food chain. Their greatest threats are humans and human activity.

Even when a bear becomes a hazard, every alternative is attempted to avoid destroying it. But if humans are at risk, there is no option. A problem bear can be a very *big* problem. The huge animals can reach a height of three or four metres when they stand on their hind legs, and adult males can weigh over 450 kilograms. The largest bear captured in the Churchill area tipped the scales at an awe-inspiring

712 kilograms. Adult females are comparably smaller, but even a small bear is a formidable adversary.

In the past, dozens of bears were killed each season. But as environmental awareness has grown, attitudes have begun to change. Polar bear hunting has been outlawed entirely since 1983. "Everyone knows a live bear is worth more than a dead bear," says Richard Romaniuk. "You can photograph a bear a hundred times, but you can only kill him once."

Today, natural resource officers have better options than killing a bear. Their number one tool is the Polar Bear Alert program. "If a bear comes into town and we're not johnny-on-the-spot already, a member of the public calls us," explains Richard. "It's like calling 911 anywhere else." Conservation officers then attempt to frighten the bear into leaving the area. They use 12-gauge shotguns, but instead of regular shells, they use firecracker shells. "When the fire-cracker blows up it makes a loud bang, and that usually gets the bear moving," says Richard. "But some bears have heard that sound often enough that they're not scared anymore, so we use another gun, like a starter's pistol. And we can fire screamers, whistlers, and bangers. This generally gets them going." They can also fire rubber slugs, causing the bear to associate the place with a distinctly unpleasant charley-horse pain, and hopefully making him want to avoid it.

Most bears promptly decide that town isn't the place for them, but each year a few take more convincing. "If a bear persists on coming into the town, at that point we have to immobilize him," says Richard. The animal is darted with a tranquilizer called Telezol, a restricted drug powerful enough to knock down a 450 kilogram bear. If the dart hits a muscle, the drug is absorbed in about five minutes, but if it hits fat, it takes about 10 minutes. The time difference can be crucial. "This time of year, we have to be very careful when darting bears," Richard adds. "Once a bear is darted his natural tendency is to run to water, but if he happens to make it to the water before the drug takes effect, he could drown." So instead of free-ranging (darting them from the ground) they use a technique called "heli-darting." They dart the bear from above, then use the helicopter to steer the bear away from water until he's down.

"Once the bear goes down we transport it to the polar bear holding compound," Richard says. "We try not to refer to it as a 'jail' because that insinuates the bears are being punished, and that's not the case." The compound was originally part of the military base, Building 20 in section D at Fort Churchill. Most people still refer to it as D20. Confinement in D20 keeps the bears away from people and people away from them. "The compound can hold 23 individuals, and last year we handled 176," says Richard. "But not 176 different bears. There were about 140 individual bears handled in 2003. If they come back a second time in the same year, they're put in the holding compound until ice forms on the bay and then released." If the facility is nearing full capacity, the bears are relocated by helicopter to an area some 65 kilometres north.

The length of time a bear remains in D20 varies. "One time we had six bear calls in town over three days. Turns out they were all for the same bear, a sub-adult 'teenager,'" says Richard. "We tried to scare her out, but she kept coming back. When we get one like this, we hold it in the compound for a 30-day time-out before release."

Occasionally a bear warrants extra-special attention. Perhaps he insists on returning or shows a tendency toward aggression. Such a bear gets a number painted on his rump. "We had one bear that was chasing vehicles in the dump," Richard recalls. "If that bear comes back we want a number on him, because his history tells us we should dart him right away. So far this year, out of 26, we've numbered one and plan on numbering two more on release."

Any time a bear is handled, Manitoba Conservation adheres to a strict protocol in conjunction with the Canadian Wildlife Service. Each new bear captured is tattooed with a number on the upper lips (or lip, if it's a cub born that year) and given ear tags with corresponding numbers. Length, girth, and fat index measurements provide an estimate of the bear's weight. All data is turned over to the Canadian Wildlife Service. "Right now the population is estimated to be around 1200," says Richard, "but we'll have a better idea at the end of next year when the CWS completes its three-year population study."

The annual gathering of polar bears at Churchill is a unique opportunity for researchers to study them and their behaviour. In fact, Canada's polar bears are among the most studied on earth, providing important insights into the bears' annual wanderings — migrations that can take individual animals across thousands of kilometres of tundra and ocean and then back again. Biologists from all over the world look to Canada for information on these animals.

Churchill's Polar Bear Alert program has worked extremely well, but Richard is quick to give credit to the townspeople. "There hasn't been a mauling or death for over 20 years," he says, "and it's because of the public's cooperation that we've been so successful." Even when he's not working directly with bears, Richard's job is still mostly about bears. Public education on bear safety is a large part of it and nothing ranks higher in importance than the pre-Halloween safety briefing for schoolchildren. They hear the same basics taught to children everywhere: stay on lighted streets and avoid dark alleys. But the kids of Churchill get something more. "I always tell them that if they see a bear they should drop their candy, because that's probably what the bear wants."

Problem bears are almost never killed anymore, but on the rare occasion it still happens. And if the bear is a mother, her death creates another problem: orphans. Polar bear cubs need their mother's care and protection until they are about a year-and-a-half, so without her they are destined to starve or be killed by predators. In the past, orphaned polar bear cubs had only two options: zoo placement or humane euthanasia.

No more. Thanks to a collaboration between Manitoba Conservation and the Born Free Foundation, a private organization in the United Kingdom, when a cub is orphaned it still has a chance at life in the wild. Born Free believes that polar bears suffer badly in zoos and so they are happy to partner with Manitoba Conservation to find an alternative. Kim Daley, now in her eighth bear season in Churchill, is a foundation researcher. She's also the on-site caregiver for a unique plan attempting to solve the problem of orphaned polar bear cubs: the Polar Bear Cub Surrogacy Program. "Born Free initiated the project as a viable option to euthanizing orphan cubs or locating them in zoos," says Kim. The concept of fostering orphan polar bear cubs illustrates how much public opinion has changed over the decades.

Inspired by the true story of Elsa the lioness, Born Free is an animal welfare and conservation charity that campaigns for the protection and conservation of animals in their natural habitat. The foundation was established in 1991 and has been instrumental in numerous projects to improve animal welfare (including Zoo Check, which monitors the welfare of animals in captivity).

Theoretically, a female bear with only one cub should be perfectly able to adopt another cub — if she can be convinced to accept it. Kim and her colleagues attempt to turn theory into practice. When an orphan is identified, officials contact Kim and the program leaps into action. "The orphan is held at the compound until a surrogate female is found," explains Kim. To maximize the chances of success, they look for a female with a single cub of similar age and size to the orphan. "We try to match the cubs as closely as possible," she adds. "Her natural cub and the introduced cub should be almost identical."

Then they use an age-old trick known to cattle and sheep ranchers everywhere: Vicks VapoRub. A generous layer of the camphor-and-menthol laden ointment on the head and neck masks all other odours, allowing the orphan to take on the familiar smells of the natural cub and making the mother more likely to accept the newcomer as her own. The biting aroma is a nice change for the humans from the bears' natural odour. What do bears smell like? "They smell bad!" Kim exclaims. "They smell like rancid fat most of the time. The best comparison would be a really bad wet dog smell. Their diet of seal is very rich in fatty acids, and mother's milk is extremely strong and rich, so the cubs have a sour smell to them. Seal is one of those smells that once you get it on you, it's hard to get it off." It's so bad that when they fly out to check up on their bears, pilots often make them leave their field jackets in the cargo area at the rear of the helicopter.

After the initial introduction period has passed successfully, the newly formed trio is released. Twenty-four hours later, Kim and her colleagues follow up on the new family. They know there are no guarantees but they always hope for the best. On a return visit after their very first adoption, they saw gratifying confirmation that polar bear surrogacy works. "We were actually able to observe the female nursing both cubs," Kim remembers. "This hadn't been documented before. Attempted adoptions hadn't been monitored by a return flight to check on them."

Their first experiment was a rousing success, but it doesn't always work so well. When Kim received a call about a nine-month-old pair of orphans, she and her co-workers immediately began searching for suitable surrogate mothers. But the ones available only had smaller cubs. They chose the closest mother-cub duos they could find, introduced the orphans, and sent them off. For several hours they monitored the expanded families closely from the ground. One mother promptly disappeared with her cubs. Subsequent search expeditions weren't able to find them, but neither did they find evidence that the adopted cub had been abandoned.

They did find the second mother and cub — but no orphan. They feared he had succumbed to a pack of wolves or perhaps an adult bear, and their fears were almost justified. "A week later he turned up in town by himself and we tracked wolves tracking him," says Kim. "He'd had a tough time of it." So they chose a different female and attempted another adoption. Once again, they set them free together in a safe location, but again, when they flew out to check on them they found the mother and her natural cub, but no orphan. "At that time the bay was frozen, and you can only fly out so far to check on them," Kim says with regret. Perhaps the mother refused to accept the newcomer; perhaps the cub refused to accept her. Perhaps he simply wandered away. In the unforgiving landscape they call home, a young bear has next to no chance of survival alone. Their best hope is that his death provided sustenance for some other animal. "The result of this," says Kim, "was the introduction to the next year's protocol of using drop-off radio collars on the females. So far, this protocol has not been tested."

The discouragement can weigh heavily at times. "We sacrifice a lot personally and professionally to do this work," Kim admits. "You can get pretty run-down. The temperatures are cold, the weather isn't always co-operative, and politics and logistics are hazards we deal with everyday." But even in the midst of disappointment and difficulty, she doesn't forget the good parts, the reasons she chose this life. "Some of the best parts of my job?" Kim doesn't even need to think about her answer. "I get to work outside and I get to spend hundreds of hours watching bears, all day long."

• • •

The people of Churchill feel strongly about the bears, too, and give their yearly visitors a warm — if watchful — welcome. Dave Daley (no relation to Kim) runs the Wapusk General Store and Wapusk Adventures in Churchill. A lifelong resident of the area, he considers polar bear encounters to be simply part and parcel of life in the north. "We don't really change our lives when the bears are here," he says. "We're just a little more cautious, I guess. My opinion is that they were here first and this is their territory. We have to let them have the right of way and try to protect them."

This laid-back attitude comes from more bear experiences than he can count. "One of my earliest memories," Dave reminisces, "is seeing my older sister meet a bear 'too close for comfort.' We used to live at Hudson's Square and my sister worked at the store. Out here, the wind is always blowing. One day she was on her way to work, walking with her head down against the wind, and I was watching her through the window. Then, there on the street, I saw a bear and she was headed right for it. I started banging on the window and yelling but she couldn't hear me because of the wind. She kept on walking and bumped right into him! She screamed, the bear ran one way, and she ran the other. Needless to say, she didn't go to work that day."

It might be an accepted part of life, but beneath his casual manner is a bone-deep knowledge of the seriousness of bear safety. Dave, who keeps and races sled dogs, takes tourists on dogsled adventures over the snow-covered tundra and out onto the ice to watch seals. During the day his dogs work hard for him, and at night they curl up snugly in the kennel Dave keeps out of town at a place called Joe Buck's Ridge. But when the dogs are in need of special care, Dave brings them to his home kennel to keep an eye on them. He'd brought one of his dogs home with him one evening, a pregnant female named Tiffany, thinking he'd be able to supervise her labour if necessary.

But at 3 a.m. Dave and his wife, Valerie, were awakened by Tiffany — and not because she was in labour. "She was barking and barking!" he recalls. Valerie prodded him to get up and find out what was wrong. He quickly threw on the first things he could find and tromped outside to investigate. Clad in nothing but cowboy boots, boxer shorts, and a jacket that was two sizes too small, he bent down on the snowy ground to quiet the dog. "That's when I heard the bear stomping and snorting behind me," he says. "I thought, 'Oh, no!' because whenever you hear that sound it's a good hint that you're way too close." Dave looked behind him and there they were, a mother bear and two cubs, barely 10 feet away from him. He dashed around the corner of the kennel and climbed up onto the deck of the house from there. When he looked down, the mother bear was standing exactly where he'd been crouching just moments before.

"My experience is not to panic when you see a bear, but when it's breathing down your neck and snorting and chomping its teeth, you want to get away as fast as you can. I'm not sure this is the right thing to do," Dave suggests with a nervous laugh, "but it seems to have worked for me so far."

He doesn't always react the same way. One day, when he'd gone outside the store to collect firewood, Valerie opened the door a crack, peeked out, and softly said, "Dave, don't look behind you. Just come inside." Naturally, he looked behind him. There, near the store and much too near him for his liking, stood a large male bear. "I continued to pick up my firewood and then came inside," he says. "Valerie asked me, 'Dave, why didn't you just drop the wood and make a dash for the door?' I told her I didn't want the bear to know I'd seen him."

During a hunting trip one summer Dave and a friend were calling for moose on the riverbank. Dave kept hearing a snorting noise that sounded suspiciously like a bear to him, but saw nothing around them. He told his friend what he thought he'd heard, but his cautions were waved away. "The next thing I know, I'm upside down with my feet up in the air. When I land, I look down and the bear's head is right between my feet!" The bear had been beneath them the entire time, in a den built into the bank. Fortunately, the bear was as frightened as they were and no one was hurt. The hunting trip, of course, continued as planned. Around the campfire that night they relived the experience, laughing shakily about their close call. "My friend said, 'I keep on seeing you on the bank! What would I have done if that bear had grabbed your leg?'"

Perhaps his many run-ins with Churchill's famous visitors have earned Dave the right to be nonchalant. Recently, at the height of the bear migration, he was awakened by the sound of "crackers." Although they were clearly coming from right next door, he wasn't alarmed. "I didn't even get out of bed to look," he says.

Chapter 7
Wildlife in the Kitchen

A t Elizabeth's Wildlife Centre in Abbotsford, British Columbia, four baby opossums hesitate at the opening of a small cardboard box. They blink their black eyes against the light, then stumble over the lip toward Elizabeth's outstretched fingers. These "joeys," rescued from the pouch of their dead mother, owe their unassuming lives to her intervention. They aren't exactly cute — they look more like small rats than anything — but they are certainly helpless. They aren't nearly ready for release into the wild yet and they still need regular, round-the-clock feedings, so instead of residing in the nursery or the clinic building, these babies live inside the house. Elizabeth has never been able to separate her life as a nurse from her work with animals.

Inside the cage on the floor of Elizabeth's spacious breakfast nook, the joeys meander obliviously amongst each other. The kitchen, it seems, is a completely natural environment as far as they're concerned. "I never cook," Elizabeth admits, "so it's a good place for them." They poke around among the straw in their cage, twitching their long noses and reaching their pink fingers toward the grapes she offers them. Although they look extremely young, she guesses that they are as old as three months. "It's deceiving," she explains, "because they spend so much time developing after birth, inside the pouch."

The gestation period for opossums is less than two weeks. At birth the babies, each the size of a navy bean, climb up through the hair on the mother's abdomen and enter the vertical opening of her pouch. Each takes one of the mother's nipples in its mouth and holds on for dear life, remaining attached for two months. As they grow and the pouch gets crowded, the babies emerge to ride on the mother's back until they are old enough to go out on their own. When Elizabeth pulled these opossum babies from the pouch of their dead mother, they were still pink, with only the slightest bit of fluff beginning to grow over their skin. Constant warmth and endless feedings were the only way to keep them alive. Now that they are mobile, furry, and eating solid food, she feels they have a good chance at making it in the wild. But they will remain with her for several more weeks at least, until she's sure they're ready.

Elizabeth is passionate about opossums. She's passionate about all the wild creatures that come through her doors. She has to be, because there's no money in wildlife rescue. But opossums have a special place in her heart.

At the back of the property is a large aviary, a holding pen where growing birds prepare for release. Elizabeth lifts the latch and walks inside. She bends down to a little shelter in the corner and calls, holding out her hand. "Here's my boy," she says, smiling. A mature opossum waddles out, stepping deliberately and slowly. He takes the morsel of fruit she offers him and continues on his way, climbing carefully up a branch onto a shady ledge on the other side of the enclosure. This fellow is her mascot. Unlike the little ones in the kitchen, he came to her as an injured adult. Because he's unlikely to survive in the wild, he'll remain with her indefinitely. He's become quite accustomed to her presence and has even become something of a "public relations" 'possum. "He comes with me when I go to the schools," Elizabeth says. "I like kids to learn about opossums because they are great animals that have a bad reputation."

About the size of an average house cat, opossums are the only true marsupial of North America and can be found throughout most of the United States and parts of Canada and Mexico. The name comes from the Algonquian Indian word *apasum*, meaning "white animal," and while there are over 65 species of opossums, only one, the *Didelphis virginiana* (or Virginia opossum, named after the state where

British colonists first saw them), is native to North America. *Didelphis*, which means "double womb," refers to the pouch where infant opossums, like kangaroos and koalas, nurse and continue their growth.

Opossums are regular visitors in urban settings, often living very near humans. They are attracted to residential areas by the availability of water, pet food left out at night, and overripe or rotting fruit that has fallen from trees. They prefer to nest in sheltered places like hollow logs, fallen trees, or burrows that have been abandoned by other animals, but they'll happily set up house beneath a sundeck or up a shade tree. A solitary, nocturnal animal, the opossum's prehensile tail and opposable thumbs make it an agile, if slow, climber. Although it does not hibernate, during very cold weather it may take refuge in a tree for several days at a time, only seeking food when hunger strikes.

These animals have little physical appeal. Although their colour, body shape, and hairless tail give them a rat-like appearance, the two are completely unrelated. Opossums actually eat rats and mice when the opportunity presents itself. When threatened, they can put on a good show, hissing, screeching, drooling, and opening their mouths widely, showing off all 50 of their teeth — more than any other North American land animal. But it's little more than a good façade. They are relatively harmless creatures whose main defence when threatened is to "play 'possum," or pretend to be dead, by rolling over, shutting their eyes, and letting their tongues loll out.

Opossums, sometimes nicknamed "nature's little sanitation engineers," have great environmental value. They are scavengers and their typical diet is opportunistically omnivorous. They'll eat anything, depending on what's available, including all types of insects such as cockroaches, crickets, and beetles. They also love snails and even help clean up carrion. Many opossums are accidentally killed on highways while attempting to feed on some other hapless animal killed by traffic. It's Elizabeth's mission to inform the public that opossums help keep neighbourhoods clean and free of harmful garden pests and unwanted rodents. Whether rural, residential, or in the wilderness, opossums are a benefit to any area they inhabit.

Elizabeth Melnick never imagined her love for wildlife would lead to the facility she now runs. She hadn't exactly intended to pursue this line of work. But in retrospect, it's a natural fit. Born with a love for all animals and trained as a registered nurse, wildlife rescue and rehabilitation work allow her to put all aspects of her skill and personality to good use.

Although she's been a licensed wildlife rehabilitator for over 18 years, she only recently gained official non-profit society status for her shelter. Now she can provide tax-deductible receipts for charitable donations and she has greater leverage for the thankless task of fundraising. But money is always an issue, although you might not guess it from the quality of her equipment. Elizabeth works in palliative care at the local

An opossum at Elizabeth's Wildlife Centre

hospital during the winter. Any time the hospital upgrades, she is given access to a host of materials deemed unusable by human standards but still perfectly usable to her: intravenous fluid pumps, incubators, hospital cribs, medical and surgical supplies, and expired medications, among other things. "They give me stuff that would either be shipped out or thrown away," she says. "It's perfect!"

Up until two years ago, Elizabeth's Wildlife Centre operated out of her home on a typical city lot in the middle of a busy subdivision. Examinations and treatments were carried out in the garage and the kitchen. The small backyard was wall-to-wall cages, and included a tiny waterfowl pond. It was tidy, clean, organized — and cramped. But it was the home where she and her husband, Bill, had raised their children and he was especially reluctant to move. Bill had lived with Parkinson's disease for many years and the house was comfortable for him.

"But he came to me one day and said, 'I don't know how much longer I'm going to be around, and I want you to be happy,'" Elizabeth remembers. So they began to watch the real estate listings. When they found their current location, they knew immediately it was perfect.

Walking up the path to the front door, visitors see a painted wooden sign that tells them they've come to the right place. "Nature's touch makes the world sing." The property features a large home on 1.11 acres of land bordered on three sides by a vast spread of designated green space. Elizabeth has room for several separate buildings, spacious flight-cages, and protected outdoor pens. "I had to take a mortgage again," she says wryly. "Our other house was paid for."

In spite of the upheaval, Bill loved the new place and was thrilled to see Elizabeth so happy. He spent hours sitting on the sundeck, just gazing at the endless view. But within a year he was diagnosed with cancer. "He always hated hospitals," Elizabeth says, "so I took care of him at home." Although it's work she's uniquely qualified for, this time it was personal. "We were married for 34 years," she says. "Bill hadn't wanted to move, but he did it for me. So I made sure he didn't have to spend a single day in hospital." In March 2003, Bill died peacefully at home.

Elizabeth shakes her head in wonder, remembering the weekend of the funeral. March is the start of her busy season but that year the phone didn't ring once. Of course she knew she could have just turned off her phone, but she couldn't stand the thought of people having nowhere to turn. "It's like somehow the word just got out, 'Don't call Elizabeth right now.'"

In the months to come, she coped with her grief by immersing herself in the care of the needy animals around her. "It saved me," she says. There was little time to think or remember. But she will always be grateful that Bill had the foresight to encourage her to pursue her dream before he died.

The larger property comes with increased expenses, but she knows she can provide better for the animals now and that's all that matters. Recently the centre received a grant of $5000 from Shell Canada and she knew exactly what to do with it. At the back of her property, near the large aviary, she's built a duck pond with a trickling waterfall, kept fresh with a pump and filter. Teals and mallards brought to her from the man-made lake in town paddle through it, completing their convalescence. Besides improving the quality of life for the waterfowl, the pond adds a sense of serenity appropriate for this wilderness retreat. But Elizabeth, who cared for over 1500 animals and birds last year, takes little time for reflection; she's got lots more plans ready for the next generous benefactor.

Wildlife in the Kitchen

She lavishes tenderness on all the patients that come through her door, but her mission is clear: to rehabilitate them and send them back to their natural environment. She handles all of them with gentle care, clucking and patting, smoothing and stroking, but they are not pets. It's essential for their survival that they remain wary of humans, so she ensures they get no more exposure than necessary and then releases them as quickly as possible.

But no matter how large and efficient her centre becomes, there will always be wildlife in the kitchen. Today, a cage with two baby cottontail rabbits sits beside the home of the opossum babies. "The rabbits are both about the same age," she says, "but they didn't come in together." One hops out toward the grass she puts in. The other stays hidden inside the little cardboard box provided for shelter. Both bunnies are barely bigger than hamsters. "I don't know about this one," she muses, scooping one shy bunny out of the box. "He came in bleeding from his nose and mouth. His eyes were all bloodshot and red and his breathing was so rattly, it sounded like he had a hole in his chest." His face is clear now though. She holds him to her ear and listens. "He sounds better," she reports. She sets him back in the cage and he hops inside the box.

Baby rabbits are notoriously fragile, with delicate skin easily pierced by the teeth or claws of cats. While they may survive a physical attack, they are particularly vulnerable to infection from their wounds. Elizabeth has a phenomenal success rate with these tiny creatures. She fully expects these bunnies to recover and estimates she'll be able to release them into the wild within another couple of weeks.

Inside her little clinic building, a domestic rabbit lies quietly in a crate in the corner, a piece of latex sewn into his skin. "He was skin and bone when he came in," says Elizabeth. "He had such a big mass in his abdomen I thought for sure it would be a tumour." But upon further exploration she found a wound, probably from a cat-bite. The wound had abscessed, creating an enormous swelling. "We drained a third of a litre of pus from that abscess," she says. The latex drain will remain in place until she's sure the infection is gone. If he recovers, Elizabeth will take him to a veterinarian to be neutered and then try to find him a home.

When domestic rabbits grow up and lose their appeal they are sometimes abandoned by careless owners to fare as best they can in the wild. Unfortunately, they don't fare well at all and usually fall prey to dogs, cats, or wild predators. Although dependent on humans for food, they can usually manage to feed themselves in the summer, but food sources become scarce in winter. Elizabeth does what she can. "Our rescued domestic rabbits are spayed and neutered to help control the unwanted rabbit population," she says. "Rabbits make wonderful pets in the right home."

• • •

Wildlife in the Kitchen

As our cities expand ever outward, many species of wildlife are displaced, forced either to relocate or to find ways of living amongst people. The Wildlife Rescue Association in Burnaby, British Columbia, deals with 3000 to 4000 birds and animals each year, many injured as a result of some sort of contact with humans. They see everything from the coyotes that skulk in the city shadows, often being hit by cars, to the tiny hummingbirds that flit boldly among the hanging flower baskets and sometimes smash into windows. "The length of time an animal stays varies a lot," says Jackie Ward, team leader of animal care. "It might be overnight or it could be several months." Because special permission is required to keep wild animals for longer than nine months, most patients are released before then. And the goal is always to get them back into their own homes as quickly as possible. The longer a wild creature is kept in captivity, the less likely its chances of successful re-release into the wild.

When they admitted a badly injured raccoon in August 2001, they weren't even sure it would survive, let alone be fit to live in the wild again. "It was a male, probably a yearling, and he'd been hit by a car," says Jackie. A severe concussion had left him blind and nearly comatose. They suspected he might have been lying injured at the side of the road for up to 12 hours before his rescue. Jackie began an aggressive treatment protocol, hoping against hope that the raccoon would recover. He needed hand-feeding three times daily and his jaw actually had to be manipulated to help him chew. He was too badly injured to be aggressive, so there was no risk to the workers of being bitten. Within a few days his appetite returned and he appeared more responsive. But he had a long way to go yet.

The raccoon had sustained a brain injury resulting in neurological damage that left him with rigidly curled, clenched paws. To counteract this muscle spasticity he was prescribed a rigorous program of physical therapy. "We'd stretch the tendons and muscles, putting him through range-of-motion exercises," says Jackie. Hydrotherapy or water exercises had long been used in human medicine; would they be helpful here? Warm water was known to increase blood circulation, and might encourage the raccoon's natural tendency to stretch his arms out and reach for objects in water. They decided to give it a try, putting him in the pool and moving his limbs. Very soon they started to see improvement. His mobility increased, he was more alert, and he responded when people entered the room. This was exactly what they were hoping for — except that it made their job more difficult. Within about a month he was exhibiting hints of the normal fear and aggression expected in a wild raccoon. "Even after he started to become more alert we kept on with the hydro-therapy for another couple of weeks," says Jackie. "Then he became too aggressive and we had to discontinue it."

They put him in a larger pen so he would have more space to move around on his own. They also consulted a herbalist, who designed a nutritional program that not only corresponded to a raccoon's diet, but also included a combination of oils and nutrients to assist in the repair of damage sustained from the accident. And a special blend of herbs was given to strengthen his immune system, increase blood flow to the brain, promote muscle fibre relaxation, and generally support the nerve tissue. As time went on, it was apparent that at least some of his vision had returned. He began walking again, slowly, and without full control of his movements at first. But his recovery continued. "After the third month," reports Jackie, "he was climbing again."

Occasionally staff members sedated him so they could give him a proper physical examination. But for the most part, their role was to allow him time to finish healing. "A lot of what we do is providing a safe place to recover, so injured animals aren't picked off by predators," says Jackie. They had specific criteria against which to judge his recovery: he needed to be able to climb, move with speed and agility, be aggressive to humans, and be able to feed himself by catching live prey. Eventually they were confident of everything but the last. He'd been at the shelter for several months, and winter had arrived. To give him the best chance of survival they wouldn't release him until spring, when food sources would be more abundant. But first they needed to be sure he could still recognize a food source when he found one.

So they put goldfish into the pond in his enclosure. With the extent of his injury, they weren't sure what to expect; any number of steps could prove problematic to him. He needed to be able to see the fish, recognize them as food, catch them without slipping and falling, and hold onto them to eat them. It was the last hurdle ... but he passed. This raccoon that had come to them near death was ready to be released back into the wild. It had taken them the better part of eight months, but they'd done it. Nearly a year after his injury, the raccoon was taken to Golden Ears Provincial Park and sent off to make his own way in the world. "We were so happy," remembers Jackie, "because a lot of times the brain damage is so bad they never recover."

Jackie loves her job. She started in wildlife rescue over seven years ago as a volunteer. After she received her Bachelor of Science in Biology, she got a full-time position at the Wildlife Rescue Association and has been there ever since. "It's so rewarding to actually be able to take care of the animals that most people never even see," she says. "But it's also the environment I work in. Everyone here is phenomenal!" She's one of three full-time and two part-time paid employees, but the centre would be lost without the 80 to 100 volunteers that help out during the course of each week. "These people are doing it because it's something they're interested in doing," emphasizes Jackie. "A lot of it is grunt work. It's dirty. It's not fun."

Sometimes it's much, much worse than that. In July 2004, North Shore Fire and Rescue called the centre about a skunk that had been found stuck in a dumpster. "It was the third time in about two years that I'd been called out to this situation," recalls Jackie. "The skunks put their heads through the drainage holes in the bottoms of the dumpsters and they get stuck. By the time we get there they've been fighting all night to get out." They estimate that if the skunk had been left another hour or two, he'd have died of dehydration. "He was so exhausted he couldn't even spray anymore," Jackie recalls ruefully. "But it still wasn't the most pleasant aroma!" At 10 a.m. it was already unbearably hot, with temperatures close to 30°C. Rotting garbage competed with the pungent odour of the struggling animal. But Jackie just plugged her nose, climbed into the dumpster, and went to work.

The first thing they did was sedate the little skunk so they could assess how badly he was lodged in place. "There was no easy way to get him out," Jackie remembers. "His head and neck were swollen by then." Another goal of sedation was to help him relax and reduce some of his pain so they could help free him. They lubricated the fur and skin around his head and neck. Then, using a piece of gauze, they wrapped his head in a sort of sling, passing it through the opening in the dumpster. "This distributes the pressure a bit more equally," explains Jackie. With gentle traction, pushing from the inside and pulling from the outside, they were finally able to free him and take a good look at his injuries. The poor fellow wasn't a pretty sight. "He was dehydrated. His head was swollen. Both of his corneas and the skin around his neck were badly abraded." They immediately removed him to the centre for first aid: subcutaneous fluids to rehydrate him, antibiotics, steroids to counteract the swelling, and ointment for his eyes.

Skunks are common visitors to the centre, especially in the summer, when staff admit one every couple of weeks. It's often the youngsters who get trapped like this. If they survive, they'll likely remember the lesson the rest of their lives. But it's frustrating for Jackie to see this type of incident over and over again. "Dumpster drainage holes are the perfect size for a skunk's head," she says. "If they could put a small bit of mesh over the openings, the problem would be solved."

Wildlife rescue and rehabilitation workers like Elizabeth and Jackie never know if the animal they save today will survive until tomorrow. Much of their work is necessary as a result of human thoughtlessness and irresponsibility. Most facilities struggle constantly to make ends meet, and the majority of their compassionate volunteers are never compensated for their time. But all of them, without fail, say their work is a reward in itself. For these dedicated people, to help one animal live as nature intended, to undo even a bit of the damage wrought by human progress, is reason enough to continue.

Chapter 8
The Last Wild Horses in Canada

The late afternoon sun slants lazily into the baked earth beneath the dry brush. Doreen and Bob Henderson park their camper near a stand of trees and stake their horses loosely nearby to rest and graze. Two massive Akitas, Japanese guard dogs, lie panting in the shade. The dogs are along for more than companionship; they run interference between their owners and wilderness inhabitants. "They've saved our lives on several occasions when we've encountered aggressive bears and moose," says Doreen.

The quarry they seek isn't as aggressive as it is elusive. They're looking for wild horses, animals that are justifiably wary of humans and could be roaming anywhere in an area roughly 325 square kilometres. Bands of these horses may be as small as three or four or as large as 18 or 20, each led by a stallion. It takes great skill to even see them, let alone get close to them, for the stallions are extremely alert. At the slightest alarm they round up their band and take them off into the trees.

In the morning, Doreen and Bob will saddle up and begin their search throughout the lonely hills southwest of Sundre, Alberta. The Hendersons, founders of the Wild Horses of Alberta Society, know that in order to advocate effectively for the protection of these magnificent animals they must know first-hand how they live. And that means trekking into the wilderness several times each year. Sometimes they ride for days without a glimpse. Other times, they get lucky.

On a recent expedition they were setting up camp and preparing to settle in for the night when something caught Doreen's eye. She paused from collecting rocks for their campfire and glanced toward their horses. That's when she saw the wary figure of a wild sorrel stallion, nose to nose with their gelding. "I shrieked," Doreen remembers. "He'd already nosed in to move the mare away." The stallion had slipped up silently, planning to steal the mare for his harem, but he bolted when Doreen yelled. Already, it appeared, this trip was a definite success.

The Hendersons have always been horse lovers, but it wasn't until 1998 that the plight of the wild horse grabbed their attention. "That's when we saw our first wild horses," says Doreen. "We just fell in love with them. They've got tails that flow down to the ground and massive manes. They don't look domestic at all. I guess they appealed to our romantic side."

There's little romance remaining in the lives of these "Spaghetti Western" remnants. Wild horses are found in 10 western states, in remote regions of Canada, and on several barrier islands off the Atlantic Coast. The United States has approximately 40,000 mustangs, officially protected there since 1971, but wild horses in Canada probably number just in the hundreds. Only the wild ponies of Newfoundland and Sable Island have protected status in Canada, and even that might be in question. On Sable Island off the coast of Nova Scotia, 200 to 350 head are protected by both limited access to the island and official regulations. These ponies have great cultural and scientific interest, but the popular notion that they are descended from shipwreck survivors is based more on romance than on reality; present-day horses came from those brought to the island between the late 1700s and the early 1900s. The Sable Island horses are entirely unmanaged and have had legal protection since 1961 under the Sable Island Regulations of the Canada Shipping Act. But this protection depends upon the horses and their habitat being monitored, as they have been since lifesaving stations (originally set up in 1801) guaranteed a continuous government presence on the island. If these government-run stations are withdrawn from Sable Island, its horses will no longer have legal protection. They will join the wild horses of western Canada in fighting for their survival.

...

The threat of animal predation is a natural part of a wild horse's life. But it isn't other wild animals that primarily jeopardize their survival. Their existence is threatened most by humans.

Wild horses are thought by some to be nuisance animals, good for nothing but target practice. Opponents claim they foul local water supplies, displace native species, and compete with domesticated cattle. They're also accused of hastening erosion by overgrazing land, and interfering with reforestation efforts by trampling or eating newly planted tree saplings. The Hendersons say wild horses are innocent of such crimes. "We've never seen evidence of this," says Doreen. "Far more damage is done by all-terrain vehicles." Wild horses can't be held responsible for overgrazing, she adds, because they're constantly on the move. Unlike fenced cattle that will stay in an area and eat until it's scoured clean, wild horses graze lightly and move on. In winter, they even help the deer and elk access food by pawing away snow from the ground. "We believe they've created a nice little ecosystem for themselves," says Doreen. "And they're prey, too. Wolf, cougar, and bear hunt them."

The slaughter of wild horses by humans has been going on unchecked for decades as they've been shot or rounded up for shipment to rendering plants. In fact, until recently there was a bounty on wild horses. But the case that spurred the Hendersons into action was a particularly grisly killing in which a horse was shot, sawed in half, and gutted. The extreme cruelty and senselessness of it lit a fire in them. "No one seemed to be doing anything to protect them," says Doreen. "The SPCA wouldn't get involved, probably because they're not considered domestic animals. Fish and Wildlife officials wouldn't get involved because they said they're not wild animals." So the wild horse fell into a grey area, with the result that they could be hunted and killed at will.

"We decided to do something instead of just complaining," says Doreen. In April 2002 the Hendersons officially established their society, to function mainly as "a lobby group trying to get some changes through the government, specifically legal protection for the horses." Ideally, the Hendersons hope for legislation similar to the Wild Horses and Burro Act in the United States. That 1971 bill states that "... wild free-roaming horses and burros are living symbols of the historic and pioneer spirit of the West; that they contribute to the diversity of life forms within the Nation and enrich the lives of the American people; and that these horses and burros are fast disappearing from the American scene." The act ensures that free-roaming horses and burros are protected from capture, branding, harassment, or death and also says these animals should be considered an integral part of the natural system of public lands.

Wild, free-roaming horses in Canada have no such protection at this time.

In British Columbia, the Chilcotin Forest District holds the other last major population of wild horses. Recent estimates indicate that there are about 400, including a large group of possibly up to 150 head in the Brittany Triangle. It's a pristine wilderness paradise, filled with lodgepole pines, spruce, aspen, sparkling lakes and streams, and abundant wildlife. The horse population appears stable, thanks in part to mild winters but mostly due to the extreme isolation of the area; it was 1973 before the first logging road reached the valley.

But the majestic trees that provide shelter for the horses also put them at risk as logging companies constantly seek new commercial stands of timber. If this continues unchecked and more forests disappear, the Brittany could be destroyed as wildlife habitat and as a refuge for some of the last wild horses of Canada. Clear-cutting, the logging practice of harvesting vast swaths of timber from a large area, exposes horses to human predation by introducing access roads and traffic, and further disrupts the natural balance by discouraging predators that help keep the horse population in check.

For wild horse advocates, the distinction between true wild horses and feral horses — those that have escaped from farms or ranches — is mainly a political one. While ranchers claim they are feral, descended from escaped settlement horses, champions of the wild horses argue that at least some of them bear genetic proof of descent from Spanish horses brought to North America by Cortez in 1519. It stands to reason that some bands will have formerly domesticated horses among them, but the majority of those observed by the Hendersons appear to have been born wild. Certainly their behaviour is that of wild animals.

Wild horse bands are usually made up of a single stallion and a group of mares and their foals, who live together year-round. Larger bands may have more than one stallion and it's not unusual to find that some stallions and their harems have been together for many years. "Even a few years ago we saw herds with 25-plus horses," says Doreen, "but not now. The numbers are going down."

Wild horses can be fiercely protective of the weak among them. They will surround an injured herd member, and even maintain a slower pace if necessary, to keep him shielded. And they're extremely solicitous of their newborns. The mortality rate for foals is high, and with a gestation period of 11 months it can take years to build up a herd.

Because of this, Doreen and Bob are always excited to see youngsters. In particular, they keep their eyes peeled for one special mare who, without fail, has a new foal every spring. They recognize her because wild horses tend to have unique colour patterns. "She's odd-looking, with a brown head and whitish grey body," observes Doreen. "You wouldn't call her pretty!" But she's healthy and strong and she's a good mother.

When male foals reach sexual maturity they are either driven out by the stallion to join bands of other bachelors, or they challenge a reigning stallion for control of a herd. Most of the time, posturing and bluffing decide the winner. But if neither contender concedes defeat, they will fight — to the death if necessary. There's no such thing as dirty fighting; they purposely aim for the vulnerable areas. A broken leg or a severed tendon means game over, and control of the harem is awarded to the winning male.

When the Hendersons saw a limping black stallion, they immediately guessed he was the loser of one such battle. "His front leg had been severely broken. It looked like he had an elbow joint high above his knee," Doreen says. They suspected the injury might have been a couple of years old. But the bone had healed enough that he could run awkwardly and was able to eat, although he was underweight. Since it's unusual for a horse to survive such an injury, they wondered how he'd managed. Then they saw his friend. "A young dun-coloured stallion stayed with him all the time, helping him eat and protecting him."

It's hard for them to see such an injury and not intervene, but they know the horses need to be left alone. They will protect them from human harm, but they also have to protect them from well-intentioned human interference. History has proven that domestication attempts can have devastating results. If the horses are captured for any reason, many will starve themselves, refusing food and water until they simply collapse. For every three captured, Doreen estimates two will die. "They just want to be free," she emphasizes. "They don't want care. They don't need rescuing."

"We go out almost every weekend," says Bob, "riding our horses and visiting and observing the 'wildies' in their natural habitat. After all these years they still get me excited as I watch in awe at their beauty."

• • •

No one has ever officially studied the wild horses of western Canada. But decades ago, when Vancouver journalist James Martindale discovered the existence of these horses, he quickly became fascinated and knew he had to learn more.

"Being a history buff, I began to think about the people who lived here on this shining, big-sky land before us. Who were they? Where did they go?" James, who lived in Alberta at the time, spent entire days in the archives of Calgary's Glenbow Museum, pouring over maps, examining old photographs, and learning about the people who first occupied this country.

He found arrowheads in the soil and, in certain spots, centuries-old teepee rings. He discovered that millions of buffalo once roamed the prairies, pursued by aboriginal hunters. "Then it dawned on me," he says. "Once upon a time, the Native peoples depended on dog power to move around the country. Dogs were harnessed to travois, dragging all the peoples' earthly possessions across the countryside. But then along came horses — and everything changed."

Full-blown horse culture had become dominant by the middle of the 19th century, explains James. Suddenly people were able to travel like the wind, hunt across wider territories, and expand ancient trade routes continent-wide. They became formidable warriors. Inter-tribal horse stealing was the greatest of adventures. Every family kept a herd of ponies, and a man with a few hundred head of horses was a very rich man. "I was hooked. I had hundreds of questions." And, as a journalist, James's motto is, "If you know how to get information, you can find out nearly anything."

He discovered that in the late Pleistocene Era, 1.8 million to 11,000 years ago, a series of devastating events killed off most of the New World's large mammals. Climatic changes and overly enthusiastic human hunters led to the extinction of the mammoth, the saber-toothed tiger, and horses. It wasn't until the 1500s that Spanish explorers reintroduced mustangs to the American continent. These horses were small and squat with long hairy manes, and were extraordinarily tough and hardy.

One of the earliest European reports associating Native peoples with horses comes from the mid-18th century journals of explorer Pierre La Vérendrye. According to La Vérendrye, at that time both dogs and horses were used only as beasts of burden. Although various tribes lay claim to being the first equestrians, the answer is lost in the mists of legend.

James was left with one big question: Where did all the

horses go? "At one time they numbered in the millions on the prairies," he says. "Where are they now? Does anyone know? Are they extinct?"

In his research, James kept coming across newspaper clippings from the 1950s and 60s highlighting the ongoing fight of activist cowboy Slim Davis to protect wild mustangs. Slim testified to the existence of a few remaining herds of purebred Spanish mustang stock still roaming the Alberta foothills, where he owned a ranch. In his lifetime, he pointed out, he'd seen many species of mountain fauna dwindle, citing the nearly lost mountain sheep as an example. He persistently claimed that "his" horses were unique, a heritage animal, and needed protection from the hunters and ranchers who were shooting them down like vermin. Authorities decried Slim as a "crank." This only made him push harder. In 1973 he took a petition to the Alberta Legislature proposing the creation of a wild horse reserve in the foothills country. His petition was barely even given an audience. But with his stubborn cowboy will still intact, Slim continued to court the media at every opportunity, hoping he might eventually grab enough popular support to make a difference.

In 1979 James crossed paths with Slim Davis. "I called him up one sunny day and asked to have a meeting with him," he recalls. "It was an offer he couldn't refuse."

Slim's Hummingbird Ranch home was in a remote area of the foothill country, accessible only by dirt roads. In this wild land without street signs, navigation is strictly by landmarks such as large rocks, fences, and trees. Based on Slim's directions, James found his way to Hummingbird Ranch. "His spread looked really lonely and rugged," he comments, as he recalls his meeting with the old cowboy — a natural charmer who loved a good story and even recited poetry when the spirit moved him. After dinner, Slim took James out into the darkness with the promise that they would see something special. "We stepped out into a stunningly fresh, starlit night," remembers James, "and walked about 30 minutes toward a corral hugging a dark forested area." Slim motioned for James to keep quiet and look in the direction he pointed. In the shadows near the far fence James discerned a hesitant, dark presence and heard a low, nickered greeting. Slowly, haltingly, a small wild mare materialized out of the shadows and approached the men. James watched in awe as the mare nuzzled Slim's outstretched hand.

"It was an 'Aha!' moment for me," says James. "Here was a man who shared my own sense of the romance of the old West. We both appreciated wild things from a distant time."

Slim's mustang mare was neither captive nor fully wild, James discovered. She dropped in and out seasonally, finding her way around the fences. Slim fed her well when she needed it, and together they developed an extraordinary, trusting relationship.

James visited Slim Davis once more, in 1980. He was determined to see more of these amazing horses. "He took me out on a ride to look for a herd of mustangs. He said very matter-of-factly that he knew their exact location." Some miles back into the foothills James and Slim located a small group of ponies grazing on bunch grass. "We approached downwind. Slim's dog gave chase, though, blowing our cover. We were within 30 metres of the horses, so I whipped out my camera. But wild mustangs don't immediately run from danger. They stand stock still, frozen. It's a well-recorded behaviour, and one that has helped to endanger them. As if caught in headlights, they're utterly vulnerable at this point. Once assured we were not going to harm them, they returned to their grazing, carefree. Dog or no dog, they had business of their own to do. We only stayed a few minutes."

Slim has since passed away, but James will never forget the sights this remarkable cowboy shared with him.

• • •

The horses of 400 years ago were very different from our modern-day horses. Those free-living mustangs descended from pure Spanish colonial stock that arrived in the 1500s and which, in turn, hailed from ancient Arab Moorish stock. Through contact with escaped domestic horses, herds grew and the mustang gene was diluted. Modern biologists are able to distinguish the mustang from "European" quarter horse stock by means of unique genetic markers.

Many wild horse bands in Alberta and British Columbia display Spanish characteristics. Some people say they show superior conformation, intelligence, and conditioning to ranch and domestic saddle horses.

Only one Canadian horse has had genetic testing done, a little dun mare owned by Steve Howlett of Cooks Creek, Manitoba.

From the moment he first saw her Steve knew she wasn't an ordinary horse, but it wasn't until much, much later — after many months of painstaking effort, phone calls, letters, and conversations — that he was able to patch together her checkered history.

In 1976, during one of the last wild horse round-ups, a dun mare was captured from a herd in the Siffleur Wilderness Area of Alberta's Kootenay Plains. Unbeknownst to her new owners, this mare, purchased for the unlikely purpose of pleasure riding, was carrying a foal of unknown sire when she left the wilderness area. "Little Orphan Annie," born in the spring of 1977, was sold to a man who ran a riding and boarding stable and had a reputation for being abusive. His harsh philosophy backfired with this filly, however, as all she did when saddled or harnessed was rebel, pinning her ears back and trying to bite.

"One day," recounts Steve, "while in harness pulling a sleigh carrying 20 people, she exploded, ripping her harness to the point where you couldn't find two pieces to stitch back together." That got her sold to an unsuspecting family who wanted a riding horse for their son. Although they treated her well, they weren't experienced enough with horses to handle

Annie, and she knew it. Since they couldn't ride her, they decided to let her have a foal and bred her to a paint stallion. Annie and her owners then moved to St. Adolphe, Manitoba.

Steve met Annie in the spring of 1984. "She was 10 months in foal and her feet had not been done in over six months," he remembers. But in spite of her untrimmed hooves and somewhat ragged physical condition, he fell in love with her immediately. It was her colour that did it. The mustang colour palette ranges from the usual solid black, brown, chestnut, and sorrel colours, to the elegant chestnut body with black mane and tail of the bay, to the flashy blonde-over-gold of the palomino. They may also have patches, blankets, or spots. Some exhibit more exotic patterns: zebra, red dun, and a pattern called *grulla*. "A *grulla* (or *grullo*, if it's a male) is usually a black horse with a dun gene," explains Steve. "In this dilution, the gene acts on the black body of the horse to make it a mousy grey colour." Each individual hair is greyish coloured, instead of the mixture of dark and white hairs seen in roans.

Steve had always loved the soft grey-brown dun colour Annie inherited from her wild mother, and in late October of that same year he became Annie's new owner. "I felt 'Annie' was not a suitable name for a horse," he says (even though he knew nothing at the time about her wild heritage), "so she was renamed Shandi." Steve's new horse had been described as a renegade, for whom the only safe place would be "in a tin." But he sensed she had been mistreated at some point, and was just misunderstood. "Shandi could be moody and always needed a good reason to do something," he concedes. "It's difficult to describe her personality accurately, as she was quite an individual, not fitting into any category." In any event, her new name, which means "mischievous one" in its original Celtic, seemed appropriate, and it stuck.

Originally from Alberta, Steve was working at the time as a guide on a Manitoba ranch. He'd recently had to relinquish his horse to a newer staff member and had no alternative but to try Shandi out at work. Few mustangs exceed 14.2 hands tall, and most weigh less than 500 kilograms. Although Shandi was big for a "wildie," she was still a fairly small horse. Steve is 6'1" tall and weighs almost 90 kilograms. He knew it would be a challenge for this little mustang to carry him. "I was worried that the long hours and constant riding would break her down," he says. "But although she lost weight no matter how well I fed her, she never missed a day of work. She was always there when I called on her, always willing."

Shandi and Steve worked 5 days a week, up to 10 hours a day, in hot and dusty or humid and bug-infested environments. She developed a reputation for being a tough, smart, fast little horse. Steve was impressed. "There wasn't much this little mare wouldn't do for me, and I really respected her." After working with her day in and day out, logging thousands of miles on her back and finding out just how resilient she was, he became curious about her history and the source of her strength.

Shandi

He was astounded when his search for her roots led him to the discovery that Shandi was a bona fide wild horse from his own home province. Eventually he became interested in pursuing the possibility that she might actually have Spanish heritage, and got in contact with the Canadian Wild Horse Society. After seeing pictures of Shandi, society representatives encouraged Steve to have her evaluated as a possible Spanish Mustang/Colonial Spanish Horse. "They sort of follow the theory that if it looks like a duck, walks like a duck, and sounds like a duck, it's probably a duck," quips Steve.

Steve hoped that Shandi could be officially registered with the American Mustang Association. The criteria are simple: confirmed birth in the wild, matching physical and temperamental characteristics, and the ability to breed true. Shandi fit on two of the three. She was the foal of a wild mare captured in an extremely remote area untouched by humans for decades. Her physique was typical of wild Mustangs of Spanish stock: small size, short back, and deep body. She also exhibited the dorsal stripe, Spanish mask face, and shoulder patch, and her spirited temperament was indicative. The only thing she hadn't done was produce a foal sired by a wild stallion, so they couldn't evaluate her ability to breed true, or to pass on these wild characteristics to a new generation.

Steve felt sure Shandi fit enough of the criteria, but would DNA testing confirm what he believed? He contacted the University of Kentucky, where genetic research was being done on wild horses, and requested a blood sampling kit. Steve duly collected the sample, completed the paperwork, and sent off the information. Then he tried to put it out of his mind. It wasn't easy. "It took months of waiting on pins and needles for the results," he says. When the results arrived, they were encouraging but not definitive. "They told me Shandi had significant Spanish Genetic Blood markers,

Andalusian being one of them."

Steve continued his pursuit for information and when he heard about the mitochondrial DNA test, he jumped on it. "All I had to do was send a sample of Shandi's mane hair, including the roots, to Germany." And ... another long wait. But this time the results were clear. Shandi had an unmistakable Iberian mtDNA pattern, the same pattern showing up in the majority of Spanish Mustangs tested in the United States.

Steve and his wife, Lynn, were overjoyed. They had been hoping the Canadian government would recognize the heritage value of Shandi and the other wild horses, so their first reaction was a feeling of vindication. But even with scientific evidence supporting the existence of Mustangs in Canada, the government has yet to take specific protective action.

Shandi (and her home herd of "wildies") are carriers of the genetic heritage of Spanish mustang stock in the Canadian wilderness. Because this has been confirmed, Shandi became the only Canadian horse registered with the American Mustang Association. "She is also the first Canadian horse registered with the Sorraia Mustang Studbook," adds Steve. "Her registry number is 'T94-C Shandi,' the 'C' standing for 'Canada.'"

A proud horse, Shandi carried herself with the dignity of one who knew her lineage. And although she became domesticated, she always retained her natural independence. "She could do it all ... good cow sense ... quiet, yet full of life ... mischievous, yet eager to please," says Steve. "In the forest she was level-headed, never shying, and wanting to lead. When you sat in the saddle it was like turning on a switch beneath you."

And just as quickly, on October 2, 2004, that switch turned off. The night before, Shandi pranced happily, awaiting her supper. "When I went to feed her in the morning," says Steve, "I found her down. Silvertip, her friend and companion for the last three years, was standing guard over her. My heart sank and I knew immediately she'd passed away. Shandi, in the last few years, never would lie down. As I entered the shelter, Silvertip nickered softly and moved away as if he knew his vigil was over. He left her in my care, watching from a respectful distance."

Shandi stirred many wild horse advocates to action, allowing people to see at close range the beauty and heritage at risk. But as public as her life had been, for Steve and Lynn Howlett the loss was personal. "Weeks after burying her, I would almost trade that legacy to have her back," Steve says. "We were privileged to have her enter our lives and are utterly heartbroken at losing her. She shall be missed."

Steve, James, Bob, and Doreen have the same questions. What do we owe these horses? Do we help them continue to exist and prosper, or do we let them perish? Are there sufficient numbers left for a healthy gene pool?

Nobody knows for sure exactly how many wild horses are left, but James says his pal Slim felt pessimistic toward the end of his life. "He thought the 1970s estimates of 'a few thousand head' were way too high. He thought a few hundred was more likely," says Jim. "Those numbers don't add up to a sustainable gene pool. I think we are seeing the last wild mustangs now before our very eyes." He adds, "Our children won't see them, ever."

Epilogue

The last rays of sunlight are dim on the horizon. Elizabeth places the carrier near a fat tree trunk and unlatches the wire door. She stands back, waiting. In a moment or two, a whiskered pink nose pokes out. Then another. Then a third. The noses are followed by beady black eyes and delicate, seashell ears. The young opossums move deliberately, sniffing their way out of the crate and into the forest.

It's been a long journey from the roadside death of their mother to the sanctuary of Elizabeth's kitchen. They understand neither the tragedy that brought them together nor the compassion of her care. There are many events Elizabeth hopes animals can't remember either. She will miss these joeys, but it's a fleeting emotion. Many other needy wild creatures, unfortunately, will arrive in the months and years ahead to take their places. But this, right now, is why she does it. All the midnight feedings, the bites and scratches, the cleaning and medicating, everything is done so the creatures she cares for might live as they were meant to live: wild.

The opossums glance in Elizabeth's direction, but only perfunctorily; their journey now is away from her care and toward a second chance at life. As they amble into the wilderness she allows herself a brief smile. And a wistful but contented sigh.

Further Reading

Wildlife Rescue Association of BC
www.wildliferescue.ca

Northern Lights Wildlife Centre
www.northernlightswildlife.com

Bowmanville Zoological Park
www.bowmanvillezoo.com

For the Birds
www.rivernet.ca/~nbiggs/

Wild Horses of Alberta Society
www.northernhorse.com

The Last of the Wild Horses, by James Martindale
http://members.shaw.ca/save-wild-horses/index2.htm

The National Wild Horse and Burro Program
http://www.wildhorseandburro.blm.gov/index.php

Acknowledgments

To the many people who generously shared their experiences with me for this book: Elizabeth Melnick, Jackie Ward, Shelley and Casey Black, Michael Hackenberger, Joan and Neil Biggs, Mike and Doreen Macri, Sam Kayra, Richard Romaniuk, Dave and Valerie Daley, Kim Daley, Bob and Doreen Henderson, James Martindale, and Steve Howlett. My sincere thanks for your enthusiastic participation! I'd also like to thank my family: Ray, Stephanie, Andrea, and Megan for caring enough to check in on me now and then and ask, "How's it going?"

A special thank you to my gifted editor, Deborah Lawson, who smoothed out the rough edges of this manuscript and is always a pleasure to work with!

Photo Credits

Cover: photos.com; Steve Howlett: page 117; photos.com: page 73; Roxanne Willems Snopek: page 90; Stephanie L. Snopek: page 125; Lisa Weir, Elizabeth's Wildlife Centre: page 15.

About the Author

Roxanne Willems Snopek lives and writes in Abbotsford, British Columbia, where she shares her home with her family and many animals, both domestic and wild. Their mountain backyard is populated with deer, squirrels, rabbits, hummingbirds, jays, songbirds of all kinds, and high above them, eagles. She knows how lucky she is.

To read more about her, see her website at www.roxannesnopek.smartwriters.com. She loves to hear from readers!

Amazing Author Question and Answer

What was your inspiration for writing these animal stories?

I'm an animal lover, of course, and I have great admiration for people who work in wildlife rescue and rehabilitation. These animals are not pets; they are not tame and the object is usually to return them to the wild. It's one thing to care for an animal that obviously adores you, like my dog. It's another thing to care for an animal that would rather remove your fingers than accept your help.

Who do you most admire in this Amazing Story?

I think Elizabeth Melnick of Elizabeth's Wildlife Centre in Abbotsford would have to be the person I most admire in this book. Because we both live in the same city, I've known about her for many years, but didn't really get to know her properly until interviewing her for this book. She's such a natural caregiver! And she never complains about the unglamorous parts of her work — she has nothing but compassion for her patients.

What part of the writing process did you enjoy most?

Visiting Elizabeth's shelter, seeing and photographing her patients up close.

Why did you become a writer? Who inspired you?

I've been an avid reader as long as I can remember but it didn't occur to me that I might be a writer, too, until I was in my twenties. I'd always kept journals, though, and during an episode of young adult career angst I remember telling a friend, "I'm going to write a book one day. I don't know what it will be about, but I know I'm going to write one.".

Who are your Canadian heroes?

Where do I start? Emily Carr, for courageously pursuing her art. Carol Shields, for writing *The Stone Diaries*. David Suzuki, for inspiring and challenging us to care for the environment. Sarah McLachlan, for music that helps me write. Emily Stowe, first Canadian woman doctor. Guy Laliberté, founder and CEO of Cirque du Soleil, the best show ever!

Which other Amazing Stories would you recommend?

I really enjoyed Susan McNicoll's *BC Murders* and *Ontario Murders*. Being a murder mystery buff, I enjoy true crime and Susan's got some great stories.

OTHER AMAZING STORIES

These titles are available wherever you buy books. If you have trouble finding the book you want, call the Altitude order desk at **1-800-957-6888**, e-mail your request to: **orderdesk@altitudepublishing.com** or visit our Web site at **www.amazingstories.ca**

New **AMAZING STORIES** titles are published every month.